The Psychology
of
Selling

HOW TO SELL MORE, EASIER, AND
FASTER THAN YOU EVER THOUGHT POSSIBLE

BRIAN
TRACY

Thomas Nelson
Since 1798

NASHVILLE   DALLAS   MEXICO CITY   RIO DE JANEIRO   BEIJING

Published in Nashville, Tennessee, by Thomas Nelson. Thomas Nelson is a registered trademark of Thomas Nelson, Inc.

Thomas Nelson, Inc., titles may be purchased in bulk for educational, business, fund-raising, or sales promotional use. For information, please e-mail SpecialMarkets@ThomasNelson.com.

Library of Congress Cataloging-in-Publication Data

Tracy, Brian.
    The psychology of selling : how to sell more, easier, and faster than you ever thought possible / by Brian Tracy.
      p. cm.
    ISBN 978-0-7852-1200-3 (hardcover)
    ISBN 978-0-7852-8806-0 (trade paper)
    ISBN 978-0-7852-7910-5 (ie)
    1. Selling—Psychological aspects. 2. Selling—Handbooks, manuals, etc. I. Title.
    HF5438.8.P75T73 2004
    658.86'01'9—dc22

                                                                                    2004026834

Printed in the United States of America

09 10 11 12 13 QW 18 17 16 15 14

This book is dedicated to my friends, colleagues, students, and practitioners of the great art of selling, to those men and women who "bravely go where no one has gone before" to make the sales upon which our companies and nations depend. You are the true heroes and heroines of our competitive enterprise system.

CONTENTS

INTRODUCTION

*The imagination is literally the workshop wherein are
fashioned all plans created by man.*
—NAPOLEON HILL

The purpose of this book is to give you a series of ideas, strategies, and techniques that you can use immediately to make more sales, faster and more easily than ever before. In the pages ahead, you will learn to get more out of yourself, and out of your selling career, than you may have ever thought possible. You will learn how to double, triple, even quadruple your sales and your income within a few months, or as little as a few weeks.

This book is the written version of my internationally successful *The Psychology of Selling* audio sales program. Since this program was originally produced, it has been translated into sixteen languages and is used in twenty-four countries. It is the best-selling professional sales training program in history.

Become a Millionaire!

According to follow-up research on graduates of the audio program, more salespeople have become millionaires by listening to and applying these ideas than by any other sales training process ever developed. Using this material, I have *personally* trained more than five hundred thousand salespeople worldwide, from thousands of companies and from virtually every industry. It really works!

My Own Story

I did not graduate from high school. Instead, as a young man, I went off to see the world. I worked at manual-labor-type jobs for a few years until I had enough money to begin traveling. I worked my way, on a Norwegian freighter, across the North Atlantic, and then traveled by bicycle, bus, truck, and train around Europe, across Africa, and eventually to the Far East. I never missed a meal, but I did *postpone* a lot of them indefinitely.

When I could no longer find a manual-labor job, in desperation, I got into sales. It seems that most of the decisions we make in life are similar to backing up in the night and hitting something, and then getting out to see what it was. In this case, for me, it was a sales job.

> **It seems that most of the decisions we make in life are similar to backing up in the night and hitting something, and then getting out to see what it was.**

Basic Training

I was hired on straight commission and got the three-part sales training program: "Here's your cards; here's your brochures; there's the door!" Armed with this "training," I began my sales career *cold-calling*, knocking on office doors during the day and knocking on residential doors in the evenings.

The person who hired me couldn't sell. But he told me that sales is a "numbers game." He said that all I had to do was talk to enough people, and eventually I would find someone who would buy. We call this the "mud against the wall" method of selling. (If you throw enough mud against the wall, somewhere, somehow, some of it will stick.) This wasn't much, but it was all I had.

Then someone told me that sales was really not a "numbers game." Rather, it was a "rejection game." The more rejections you collect, the more sales you are likely to get. Equipped with this advice, I ran from place to place so I could get rejected more often. They said that I had the "gift of gab," so I used it. When a person seemed uninterested, I would speak louder and faster. But even though I hurried from prospect to prospect, and spoke louder and faster to each person, I was barely holding on by my fingernails.

The Turning Point

After six months of struggling, making just enough sales to pay for my single room in a small guesthouse, I finally did something that changed my life: I went to the most successful guy in our company and asked him what he was doing differently from me.

I wasn't afraid of hard work. I would get up at five or six in the morning, prepare for the day, and be waiting in the parking lot at 7:00 AM when my first prospects came to work. I worked all day long, going from office to office and company to company. In the evenings, I would knock on residential doors until nine or ten at night. If the light was on, I would make the call.

The top salesman in my office, who was only a couple of years older than me, had a completely different approach. He would roll into the office about nine o'clock. A few minutes later, a prospect would come in, and they'd sit and talk. After a few minutes' conversation, the prospect would take out his checkbook and write a check for our product.

The salesman would then go out that morning and make another couple of sales, and then have lunch with another prospect. In the afternoon he would make another couple of sales and then perhaps have a drink or dinner with another prospect. He was selling five and ten times as much as me, or anyone else in our office, and he hardly seemed to be working at all.

Training Makes the Difference

It turned out that he had worked for a Fortune 500 company when he was younger. That company had spent sixteen months training him intensively in the process of professional selling. With those skills he could then go to work for any company or industry and sell any product or service in virtually any market. Because he knew how to sell, he could sell circles around people like me, even though he was working half the time or less. This discovery changed my life.

When I asked him what he was doing differently, he said, "Well, show me your sales presentation, and I'll critique it for you."

That was my first problem. I had no idea what a "sales presentation" looked like. I had heard that there was such a thing, but I had never seen one myself.

I said, "You show me yours, and I'll show you mine."

He was patient and polite. He said, "OK, here is a basic sales presentation from beginning to end." He then walked me, step-by-step, through a sales presentation for our product.

Instead of using a "speech" or clever one-liners to get attention or to overcome resistance, he asked a series of logical questions, from general to specific, that were ideally suited to a genuine prospect. At the end of this series of questions, it had become perfectly clear to the prospect that he could use and benefit from our product. The final question was simply to close the sale.

Take Action Immediately

I wrote everything down. Fortified with this new approach to selling, I went out and started calling on prospects once more. But this time, instead of *talking*, I asked *questions*. Rather than trying to overwhelm the prospect with the features and benefits of my product, I focused on learning about the prospect's situation and how I could best help him or her. With this new method, my sales went up.

Then I learned about *books* on selling. I had no idea that some of the best salespeople in the world had written some of the best ideas on selling in *books*. I began reading everything I could find on selling, spending the first two hours of every day studying and taking notes.

Next I learned about *audio learning*. It changed my life. I began to listen, hour after hour, to audio programs as I walked from office to office. I listened to them in the morning; I listened to them in the evening. I rehearsed and practiced the best sentences and phrases from the best salespeople until I could recite them in my sleep. And my sales went up and up.

Then I discovered *sales seminars*. I thought I had died and gone to heaven. I had no idea how much you could learn from a sales seminar. I began to take every seminar and course I could find, even if I had to travel long distances, which I did, and which I could eventually afford to do. And my sales continued to increase.

Moving into Management

My sales were so high that my company made me a sales manager. They said, "Whatever you're smoking, find some people who want to get into sales and share it with them."

I began to recruit salespeople off the street and through newspaper ads. I showed them my methodology and process of selling. They walked out the door and began making sales immediately. Today, many of them are millionaires and multimillionaires.

Be the Best

The simple idea that changed my life was the discovery of the "Law of Cause and Effect." What this law says is that there is a cause for every effect,

xiv   THE PSYCHOLOGY OF SELLING

that everything happens for a reason. Success is not an accident. Failure is not an accident either. In fact, success is *predictable*. It leaves tracks.

> **Success is not an accident. Failure is not an accident either. In fact, success is predictable. It leaves tracks.**

Here is a great rule: "If you do what other successful people do, over and over again, nothing in the world can stop you from eventually getting the same results that they do. And if you don't, nothing can help you."

Remember that everyone in the top 10 percent in sales today started in the bottom 10 percent. All who are now doing well were once doing poorly. Everyone at the front of the line of life started at the back of the line. And in every case, what these top people did was *learn from the experts*. They discovered what other top people were doing to be successful, and they did the same things themselves, again and again, until they got the same results. And so can you.

Use What You Learn

Sometimes I ask my sales audiences, "What is the most popular piece of home exercise equipment in America?" After a little hesitation, I tell them: it's the *treadmill*. Americans spend more than one billion dollars on treadmills every single year.

Then I ask a second question: "If you buy a treadmill and take it home, what will determine how much benefit you get from that treadmill?"

They answer, "The benefit you get will depend on how often you use it and how long you use it each time."

Here's my point. There is no question about whether or not the treadmill will give you the results you seek. That has already been established. Everyone knows that if you use a treadmill regularly and for an extended period of time, you will get definite health benefits.

The strategies and techniques you will learn in this book are very much like a treadmill. There is no question about whether or not they work. They are used by all the highest-paid salespeople in every industry worldwide. They are tested and proven. The more you use these methods, the better you will get at them and the better and faster results you will achieve. By practicing what you learn in the pages ahead, you will move into the top 10 percent of sales professionals in your field and become one of the highest-paid people in the world.

Is this a good goal for us to achieve together? If you feel it is, let's get started.

Whatever the mind of man can conceive and believe, it can achieve.
—NAPOLEON HILL

THE INNER
GAME OF SELLING

Visualize this thing that you want. See it, feel it, believe in it.
Make your mental blueprint, and begin to build.
—ROBERT COLLIER

Nothing happens until a sale takes place. Salespeople are some of the most important people in our society. Without sales, our entire society would come to a grinding halt.

The only real creators of wealth in our society are *businesses*. Businesses produce all products and services. Businesses create all profits and wealth. Businesses pay all salaries and benefits. The health of the business community in any city, state, or nation is the key determinant of the quality of life and standard of living of the people in that geographical area.

You Are Important

Salespeople are the most vital people in any business. Without sales, the biggest and most sophisticated companies shut down. Sales are the spark plug in the engine of free enterprise. There is a direct relationship between the success of the sales community and the success of the entire country. The more vibrant the level of sales, the more successful and profitable is that industry or area.

Salespeople pay for all the schools, hospitals, private and public charities, libraries, parks, and all good things that are vital to our standard of living. Salespeople—through their sales and the profits and taxes created by successful companies—pay for government at all levels, for all welfare, unemployment insurance, social security, Medicare, and other benefits. Salespeople are essential to our way of life.

Salespeople Are the Movers and Shakers

President Calvin Coolidge once said, "The business of America is business." If you strip down the major newspapers, like the *Wall Street Journal* and *Investor's Business Daily*, and the major business magazines, such as *Forbes, Fortune, Business Week, Inc., Business 2.0, Wired,* and *Fast Company*, almost everything they write about has something to do with sales. All of our financial markets, including the prices of stocks, bonds, and commodities, as well as current interest rates, have to do with sales. As a professional salesperson, you are a "mover and shaker" in our society. The only question is, how well do you sell?

For many years, sales was considered to be a second-rate occupation. Many people were embarrassed to tell others that they were in sales. There was a general bias against salespeople. Recently, the president of a Fortune 500 company told a journalist, "Around here, we consider sales to be the sleazy side of our business."

The Best Companies

This attitude is changing quickly. Today, the very best companies have the very best salespeople. The second-best companies have the second-best salespeople. The third-best companies are on their way out of business. The most successful organizations in the world are all superb selling organizations.

Hundreds of universities now offer courses in professional selling, a great change from a few years ago. Many young people are coming out of college and immediately seeking positions in sales with large companies. More CEOs of Fortune 500 companies have come up through the ranks from sales than from any other part of the company.

More CEOs of Fortune 500 companies have come up through the ranks from sales than from any other part of the company.

The most powerful businesswoman in America today is Carly Fiorena, president and CEO of Hewlett Packard. After obtaining a degree in medieval history from Stanford, she went to work at AT&T in sales and worked her way up. Pat Mulcahy, the president of Xerox, also worked her way up from sales. Many of the top companies in the world are headed by former salespeople.

High Income and Job Security

You can be proud to be a sales professional. Your ability to sell can give you a high income and lifelong job security. No matter how many changes take place in the economy, there will always be a need for top salespeople. Regardless of how many companies and industries become obsolete or just go out of business, good salespeople will always be in high demand. By becoming excellent in sales, you can accomplish any financial goal you set for yourself.

Seventy-four percent of self-made millionaires in America are entrepreneurs, people who start and build their own businesses. They get an idea for a product or service that no one else is offering, or which they feel they can offer better than the competition, and they start their own businesses. And among entrepreneurs, the single most important skill for success is the ability to sell. Every other skill can be hired away from someone else. But the ability to sell is the key factor determining a company's success or failure.

Five percent of self-made millionaires in America are salespeople who have worked for other companies all their lives. Salespeople today are some of the highest-paid people in America, often earning more than doctors, lawyers, architects, and persons with extensive academic degrees.

Sales is a gainful profession. In sales, there is no ceiling on your income. If you are properly trained, are skilled, and are selling the right product in the right market, there is no limit to the amount of money you can make. Selling is the only field in our society where you can start with little skill or training, come from any background, and be making a great living in a matter of three to twelve months.

The 80/20 Rule in Selling

When I started selling, someone told me about the Pareto principle, also known as the 80/20 rule. He said, "The top 20 percent of salespeople make 80 percent of the money, and the bottom 80 percent only make 20 percent of the money."

Wow! I was young, and this was a real eye-opener for me. I made a decision, right then, that I was going to be in the top 20 percent. Later I learned that this was one of the most momentous decisions and turning points of my life.

Again, the top 20 percent of salespeople make 80 percent of the sales and 80 percent of the money. The bottom 80 percent of salespeople only make 20 percent. Your mission is to *decide* to join the top 20 percent, and then to *learn* how to get there.

The Pareto principle also applies to the top 20 percent of salespeople. It says that the top 20 percent of the top 20 percent, which equals the top 4 percent, earn 80 percent of the money in the top 20 percent of salespeople. Wow! In every large sales force, four or five people out of one hundred make as many sales and earn as much money *as all the rest put together.*

Never Worry About Money

There is a very good reason to get into the top 20 percent, and then later, into the top 4 percent: you will never have to worry about money again or fret about job security. You'll never lose sleep over employment. The people in the top 20 percent or better are some of the happiest people in our society.

On the other hand, the people in the bottom 80 percent are worried about money. One of the great tragedies of our society, the most affluent in human history, is that the majority of people worry about money most of the time. They get up in the morning thinking about their money problems. They think about how little money they have all day long. When they come home at night, they talk and often argue about money and how much everything costs. This is not a good way to live.

Top People Earn Vastly More

The people in the top 20 percent, on average, earn sixteen times the average income of the people in the bottom 80 percent. Those in the top 4 percent earn on average sixteen times that of the folks in the bottom 20 percent. This is astonishing!

A large American insurance company tested this 80/20 rule some years ago with their several thousand agents nationwide. They discovered that they had individual agents throughout the country who alone were selling and earning more than twenty to thirty other full-time, trained, professional agents, even though they were all selling the same products to the same people, at the same prices out of the same offices, under the same competitive conditions.

In the same year, I addressed two elite groups in two different industries. The people in these industries had all started off on the street, dialing for dollars out of the newspaper or the Yellow Pages. They all worked on straight commission, one sale at a time. But the average yearly income of the salespeople in these elite groups was $833,000 and $850,000. Some of the top people in these groups earned several million dollars a year on straight commission!

Your goal must therefore be to get into the top 20 percent, and then the top 10 percent, the top 5 percent, the top 4 percent, and so on. The purpose of this book is to get you there. It is to take you from wherever you are today to wherever you want to go in the future. It is to make you one of the highest-paid people in your industry.

The Winning Edge

If the top 20 percent of salespeople in an industry earn 80 percent of the money, and the top 20 percent of companies in an industry earn 80 percent of the profits, what are the distinguishing factors of these individuals and organizations that make such an incredible difference possible? The conclusion is that they have developed the *winning edge* in their fields.

This *winning edge concept* is one of the most important management and sales ideas of the twenty-first century. This principle says, "Small differences in ability can lead to enormous differences in results." The difference between the top performers and the average or mediocre performers is not a huge difference in talent or ability. Often, it is just a few small things done consistently and well, over and over again.

Win by a Nose

For example, if a horse runs in a race and wins by a *nose*, it wins ten times the prize money of the horse that loses by a nose. Here's the question: Is the horse that wins by a nose ten times faster than the horse that loses by a nose? Is it 10 percent faster? No. It is only a nose faster, but that translates into a 1,000 percent difference in prize money.

If a salesperson gets the sale in a competitive market, does it mean that he or she is ten times better than the salesperson who lost the sale? Of course not! Sometimes it is only a small technicality that causes a customer to buy from one person rather than another. The fact is, the salesperson who wins the sale may be only a "nose" better than the one who loses it.

Salespeople have a disadvantage over horses. There are no consolation prizes. If a horse comes in second or third, he still comes in "in the money." But in selling it is a "winner take all" transaction. The salesperson who loses the sale gets nothing, no matter how many hours he or she has invested in developing the sale.

Become a Little Bit Better

In selling, you only have to be a *little bit* better and different in each of the key result areas of selling for it to accumulate into an extraordinary difference in income. A small increment of skill or ability, just 3 or 4 percent, can give you the winning edge. It can put you in the top 20 percent, and then the top 10 percent.

> In selling, you only have to be a little bit better and different in each of the key result areas of selling for it to accumulate into an extraordinary difference in income.

Once you develop this small lead, like compound interest, it continues to grow. At first, you move slightly ahead of the crowd. As you use your additional skills, you get better and better at them. The better you become, the better results you get. You soon begin to pull ahead of the crowd by a larger and larger margin. In a few years, or even a few months, you can be earning five or ten times as much as others who are still performing at average levels.

Characteristics of Top Salespeople

There are certain characteristics that separate successful salespeople from average salespeople. These qualities have been identified over the years through interviews, surveys, and exhaustive research. We also know two things: First, no one is *born* with these qualities. Second, all of these qualities are *learnable* through practice. *You* can develop the characteristics that will virtually guarantee an extraordinary quality of life for yourself.

It was once believed that people were successful because they came from the right families, had the right educations, developed the right contacts, got good grades in school, and other measurable factors. But then researchers discovered that there were people who started with none of these advantages, yet ended up at the top of their professions.

Starting from Nothing

One of the best proofs of this is the number of new immigrants who arrive in this country with little money, no contacts, no school or university background, limited English skills, and every other conceivable disadvantage. But somehow, in a few years, they have overcome every single difficulty and have become leaders in their field.

In my seminars, I continually meet men and women from all over the world who came to this country with nothing and who are now top salespeople, highly paid, and even self-made millionaires. In every case, the reasons have more to do with what is going on *inside* of them than with what is going on *outside*.

Success Is Mental

It is what goes on inside the *mind* of the salesperson that makes all the difference. Some years ago, Harvard University did a study of sixteen thousand salespeople and found that the basic qualities that determine success or failure in selling were all *mental*. If a person had certain qualities, he or she would succeed, holding constant for everything else. If you develop these psychological qualities, they then form the foundation for your own personal sales success.

If you want to know how tall a building is going to be, you look at how deep they dig the foundation for that building. The deeper the foundation, the taller the building. In the same way, the deeper *your* foundation of knowledge and skill, the greater the life that you will be able to build.

Once you have built your foundation and have become absolutely excellent at selling, you can go anywhere and write your own ticket. And you can always build your foundation deeper.

Use More of Your Potential

The average salesperson uses only a small percentage of his potential for effectiveness in selling. It is estimated that the average person in general never uses more than about 10 percent of his potential. What this means is that each person has at least 90 percent or more potential left untapped. It is when you learn how to unlock this additional 90 percent of your own potential that you move yourself into the income categories of the highest earners.

Follow the Leaders

If your goal is to be in the top 10 percent of salespeople in your field, the first thing you do is find out who is already in the top 10 percent. Instead of following the followers, the average performers in your business, follow the *leaders.* Compare yourself to the top people. Remember, *no one is better than you, and no one is smarter than you.* If someone is doing better than you, it just means that he or she has discovered the cause-and-effect relationships in selling success before you have.

British philosopher Bertrand Russell once said, "The very best proof that something can be done is that someone else has already done it." This means that if someone else is earning five or ten times as much as you, this is evidence that you can earn the same amount if you simply learn how. Remember, everyone starts at the bottom and works his way up. If someone is doing better than you, find out how he got from the bottom to where he is today. Sometimes the very best way to find this out is to go and ask him. He will probably tell you. Top people are usually willing to help other people who want to succeed.

Your Master Program

The most noteworthy breakthrough in psychology and human performance in the twentieth century was the discovery of the *self-concept*. Your self-concept is the bundle of beliefs that you have about yourself. It is the way you see yourself and think about yourself in every area of your life. Your self-concept is the "master program" of your subconscious computer. It is like an operating system that determines everything you say, think, feel, and do.

There is a direct relationship between your self-concept, on the one hand, and your performance and effectiveness, on the other. You always perform on the *outside* in the manner consistent with your self-concept. All change/improvement in your life begins when you alter and improve your self-concept, your inner programming.

Not only do you have an overall self-concept that determines how you think and feel generally about yourself, your life, and other people, but you also have a series of "mini self-concepts." These are little self-concepts that determine your effectiveness and performance in each area of your life, from riding a bicycle to making a speech.

Your Self-Concept in Selling

For example, in selling you have a self-concept with regard to yourself and prospecting. If you have a high, positive self-concept, then prospecting is no problem for you. You get up in the morning eager to call on new people. You are competent and confident in the area of prospecting, so your sales pipeline is always full.

If you have a poor self-concept with regard to prospecting, you will approach prospecting with fear and anxiety. You will avoid it wherever possible. The very idea of prospecting will make you tense and uneasy. You will do as little of it as possible and continually look for ways to avoid the activity. This is true in every other area of selling as well.

What Determines Your Income

Every salesperson already has a self-concept for the amount of money that he or she earns. Psychologists have found that you can never earn 10 percent more or less than your self-concept level of income. If you earn 10 percent more than you think you are entitled to, you will immediately engage in *compensating* behaviors to get rid of the money. If you have a great month and earn *more* than you had expected, you will have an irresistible urge to spend it on dinners, travel, clothes, or something else. It will burn a hole in your pocket.

If you earn 10 percent or more *below* your self-concept level of income, you will engage in *scrambling* behaviors. You will start thinking about working longer, harder, smarter, better, in order to get your income back up into your "comfort zone." Once you get into your comfort zone, you will relax and breathe a deep sigh of relief.

Change Your Comfort Zone

The only way you can increase your sales income is by expanding your comfort zone with regard to the amount you earn. Some people have a comfort zone of $50,000 a year. At that level, they relax and coast. Others have a comfort zone of $100,000 a year. That is the level that they strive toward, and they only relax when they hit that target.

Here is the cosmic joke: there is usually very little difference in talent between the person who earns $50,000 per year and the one who earns

$100,000 per year. The only difference is that one has settled at a lower level while the other has refused to settle for less than $100,000.

Reset Your Financial "Thermostat"

You can never earn more on the outside than you can on the inside. It is almost as if you have an "income thermostat" that determines your financial temperature. As you know, when a thermostat is set at a certain temperature, it will continually adjust the heating and cooling to keep the room at that temperature. In the same way, if you see yourself as a $50,000-a-year person, you will continually engage in behaviors that keep your income at $50,000.

> **You can never earn more on the outside than you can on the inside. It is almost as if you have an "income thermostat" that determines your financial temperature.**

In my seminars and in my work for corporations, I constantly run into this strange phenomenon. A salesperson will set a goal to earn $50,000 or $60,000 in the course of the year. But then he has a great year and hits the $50,000 mark by the end of September. Suddenly, for some reason, the sales dry up. He stops selling for the rest of the year. He cannot seem to get himself motivated, no matter how good the market is for his product. He spins his wheels until December 31. Then, on January 1, he is out of the gate like a horse at a horse race, and selling again. In every case, it is his self-concept.

Sometimes people set a goal to earn a certain amount in a particular month. But if they have a great month and they earn their self-concept amount by the middle of the month, they stop selling for the next two weeks. They can hardly wait until the first of the month so they can psychologically get themselves back into selling. This is quite common.

Break Free of the Past

Many people hold themselves back because they think that it is not right for them to earn more than their *fathers.* Time and time again, I have seen salespeople who plateau at a certain income level because that is the highest amount that their fathers ever earned. At an unconscious level they have decided that they *do* not earn more than that amount. And this becomes true for them.

In an extreme case I saw, a young man moved from the farm into the city and got a job selling satellite dishes to farmers. This salesman came from a poor background and had never earned very much money. But the harvest was good that year, and the farmers were buying $5,000 satellite dishes with both hands. He began making money faster than he had ever dreamed in his life.

But the experience of making so much money so quickly was so traumatic for him that after a couple of sales at the beginning of the week, he would actually go home, turn off all the lights in his small apartment, crawl under the covers in his bed, and lie there in the dark with his heart pounding. He was so far out of his self-concept range of income that the stress was overwhelming him.

Change Your Mind

To increase your income, you must achieve your financial goals *in your mind* before you can ever achieve them in your reality. Your aim should be to increase your self-concept level of income bit by bit until you think, see, and feel yourself as a higher-income earner.

Imagine yourself as if you were *already* the kind of person you want to be, earning the kind of money you want to earn. Look at other people who are earning more money than you and imagine that you are exactly like them. Suppose that you are already financially independent. Picture yourself having all the money you will ever need and only making sales calls because you enjoy meeting new people. This calm, confident, relaxed attitude, as if you were already a wealthy person, will help you perform at your very best, with much less tension.

Be Realistic

It is important to be realistic in developing your new self-concept, especially at the beginning. When I first learned about the power of the self-concept and how my self-concept controlled my income, I was earning about $30,000 a year. I immediately set a goal to earn $300,000 a year. But instead of this big goal *motivating* me, it actually served as a *demotivator*. As opposed to my mind going to work to find a way to earn that kind of money, my mind shut down, like turning off a light switch.

What I learned later was that a goal that is vastly beyond anything you have ever accomplished before is *ignored* by your self-concept. Instead of motivating you, it discourages you. After six months of working toward this new, unrealistic goal, I finally realized my mistake and reset my goal for $50,000 per year. Almost immediately, I began making progress and had soon achieved my new goal.

Your Income Level Locks In

Here is another interesting point. A salesperson may start off at the bottom and work his way up over a period of several years, eventually earning more than $100,000 a year. But then the economy goes south, the industry retracts or shuts down, and he has to start over with a different company selling a different product. How much do you think he earns in the following year? Answer: more than $100,000.

Why is this? Because he already has a self-concept as a $100,000-a-year salesperson; no matter what happens on the outside, he will always find a way to earn $100,000 or more.

You've read stories of senior executives with large corporations who are earning more than a million dollars a year. For some reason, they lose their jobs. Then, a couple of months later, you read or hear about them and learn that they are working for another company and *still* earning more than a million dollars a year. The fact is, once a person is a *million-dollar-a-year* person, no one would think of offering him or her less. It is all a matter of self-concept.

The Key Result Areas of Selling

In selling, there are seven *key result areas*, or *KRAs*. These KRAs are like the digits in a telephone number. You must dial each of them in sequence if you want to get through and make a sale. Your performance and effectiveness in each of these key result areas determine your overall success and the height of your income.

These seven key result areas are *prospecting, building rapport, identifying needs, presenting, answering objections, closing the sale,* and *getting resales and referrals.* Your self-concept in each of these seven areas determines your performance in these areas, as well as your overall income level.

Fortunately, everyone who is good in any one of these areas was once poor at it. Every professional in the top 10 percent started in the bottom 10 percent. The good news is that, if you can drive a car or operate a cell phone, you can become excellent in each of these seven critical skills. It is simply a matter of learning and practice.

If you have a poor self-concept with regard to any particular sales activity, you will avoid that activity whenever possible. But the only reason that you fear taking action in a particular skill area is because you are not good at it—*yet.* You have not yet mastered the skill. If you are not good at something, you will make mistakes. You will feel awkward, angry and frustrated. It would be normal and natural for you to avoid that activity.

Master the Skill

The solution for your fears or reluctance in any key skill area in selling is for you to master that skill. Fortunately, there are more books, audiotapes, courses, and bits of advice available to you now to help you master each skill than you could consume in a lifetime. There is absolutely no reason for you to be held back from joining the top 10 percent simply because you are weak in a particular skill area.

You can learn how to prospect effectively. You can be taught how to build high levels of rapport and trust with prospects. You can become skilled at how to ask questions and listen carefully to the answers. You can develop calmness and confidence in your interactions with others. You can learn anything you need to learn through practice and repetition.

It is the same with each skill area. You can become an expert at accurately identifying the needs of the person you are talking to, and qualifying the prospect, by asking more and better questions.

You can become excellent in your sales presentation, growing so effective that people are tearing the product out of your hands even before you finish talking.

You can learn how to answer the prospect's objections and concerns, responding so satisfactorily that the objections disappear and never come up again. You can learn the various methods included in this book for asking for the order and closing the sale at the appropriate time.

Finally, you can learn how to create a "golden chain" of referrals from prospects and customers and how to sell more and more to people who have bought from you already. These are all learnable skills.

Get Better at What You Do

The better you get in any area, the more positive your self-concept becomes in that area. The more confidence you have in your ability, the happier you feel when you are doing that part of your job, and the better results you will get. You can, in fact, like a sculptor, shape the entire quality of your sales personality.

You never feel uneasy doing something that you are good at. You only feel anxious doing something that you *think* you are not particularly good at. Every single step that you take to improve in any area raises your self-confidence and increases your likelihood of success each time you try it.

Face Your Fears

When you start selling for the first time, your heart is usually in your throat. It is pounding so loudly that you think people around you can hear it. Your stomach is often churning when you go into your first sales call. Psychologists say that you often act as if you were a child in fear of getting a spanking.

Your self-concept is largely subjective. It is not based on reality. It is based solely on the ideas or thoughts that you have about yourself, especially the self-limiting opinions that hold most people back.

Fear and self-doubt have always been the greatest enemies of human potential. Many people doubt their ability to excel in a particular area, and even though it is not true, it *becomes* true. As William James of Harvard said, "Belief creates the actual fact." If you believe that you are limited in some way, you will feel and act as if you are limited, and it will become true for you.

> **Fear and self-doubt have always been the greatest enemies of human potential.**

Don't Sell Yourself Short

Some people feel that they are terrible at closing sales. As long as you think that and say it to yourself, then you will be terrible at closing sales. The very idea of asking for the order will cause your heart to pound, your stomach to churn, your palms to sweat, and your mind to go blank. The fact is that closing is a normal and natural end of a sales conversation, as you will learn. Once you have mastered the art of closing sales, you will be able to ask for the order under any circumstances.

Some people are convinced that they are terrible on the phone. Because of the common fear of rejection, they avoid calling people who may not be friendly and welcoming. They then say to themselves, "I hate calling strangers."

As long as you think and say this to yourself, every time you pick up the phone, you are going to stumble over your words. You will make mistakes and perform poorly.

Challenge Your Self-Limiting Beliefs

The good news is that your self-limiting beliefs are usually based on erroneous information. They are not based on fact or reality. They are very often illusions in your own mind. Because they are unreal, you can get rid of them by replacing them with new, positive beliefs of confidence and competence in any area.

Self-limiting beliefs develop early and easily. Sometimes you will try something, like skiing or skating, and do it poorly the first time. You will immediately conclude that you are no good at that sport. From then on, you will sabotage yourself by seeking out examples to validate your initial decision. Soon you will avoid that area of activity altogether.

Louise Hay, the teacher and metaphysical writer, says that the core problem that each person has is the feeling of "I'm not good enough." We all have the feeling, deep down inside, that we are not as good as other folks. We feel that people who are doing better than us *are* actually better than us. If they are *better* than us, we unconsciously conclude, we must be *worse* than they are. If they are worth more, then we must be worth less. This false conclusion is the fundamental cause of most unhappiness in our society.

The Reactor Core of Your Self-Concept

The most important discovery of all in self-concept psychology is the central role of your *self-esteem*. Your self-esteem is best defined as "how much you like yourself." How much you like yourself is the critical determining factor of your personality and of everything that happens to you.

The degree to which you like yourself in any area is the key determinant of your performance and effectiveness in that area. It determines how much money you make, how you dress, how well you get along with other people, how much you sell, and the quality of your life.

A person who really likes himself or herself has high self-esteem and therefore a positive self-concept. When you really like yourself in a particular role, you perform at your best in that role.

The more you like yourself, the more you like other people. The more you like other people, the more they like you in return. The more you like your customers, the more your customers like you, and the more willing they are to buy from you and to recommend you to their friends.

High-self-esteem people meet and marry other high-self-esteem people. High-self-esteem parents raise high-self-esteem children. High-self-esteem bosses build high-self-esteem salespeople and employees. High-self-esteem men and women set higher standards for themselves and practice higher levels of self-discipline. They have better friendships and get along better with the people they meet. They are generally happier and more fulfilled than people who don't like themselves very much.

Self-Esteem and Sales Performance

The more you like yourself in prospecting, building rapport, identifying needs, presenting your product or service, answering objections, closing the sale, and getting resales and referrals, the better you will be in each of these areas.

A person who doesn't like himself or feels badly about himself in a particular area performs poorly in that area. Low-self-esteem salespeople who don't like themselves, don't like other people very much either. As a result, they have a hard time building high-quality relationships with customers. For some reason, customers don't particularly like or trust them and prefer to buy from someone else.

How much you like yourself is the key determinant of your success in sales *and* of your income. As a matter of fact, it determines how successful you are in every part of your life.

The Great Discovery

Because of the power of your mind in determining your life and destiny, one of the greatest discoveries in history is that *you become what you think about most of the time.*

Happy people think happy thoughts. Successful people think successful thoughts. Loving people think loving thoughts. Wealthy people think wealthy thoughts. They become what they think about most of the time.

In addition, you become what you *say to yourself* most of the time. Successful people control their inner dialogues. They talk to themselves positively and confidently as they go through their days. Perhaps the most powerful words you can say to yourself to build your self-esteem are "I like myself!"

Successful people control their inner dialogues.

Each time you say, "I like myself!" your self-esteem goes up. When you repeat the words "I like myself!" over and over throughout the day, you actually cause a chemical change in your brain. You release endorphins that give you a general feeling of confidence and well-being. The more you say, "I like myself!" the more confident you feel and the more competently you perform.

Be Your Own Cheerleader

When I learned this affirmation many years ago, I used to repeat it to myself ten, twenty, and even fifty times per day. I would say it in the morning and in the evening. I would say it as I drove along and before every sales presentation. I would keep repeating it until I drove the message deep into my subconscious mind, where it "locked in" and took on a power of its own. You can do the same thing.

Every time you say, "I like myself!" your overall self-concept improves. Your ability to perform and your level of effectiveness increase immediately. You do everything, including selling, better when you have a high level of self-generated self-esteem.

The Best Time to Make a Sale

Here's a question for you: When is the best time to make a sale? Answer: right *after* making a sale. Why? Right after you make a sale, your self-esteem soars. You feel terrific about yourself as a salesperson. You like yourself more. You feel like a winner. When you walk in to speak to the next prospect, feeling terrific about yourself, you will perform at your very best. There will be something about you that has a powerful effect on the customer. Your positive attitude and confident bearing will trigger a desire, at a subconscious level, to buy from you.

Sometimes a salesperson will make a sale first thing in the morning, and then another, and then another and another and another, and sell more in a single day than he or she might have sold in a week or two. This spike in sales performance has nothing to do with the product, the market, or the customer. It happens because the seller's self-concept has gone up like the mercury in a thermometer on a hot day. As a result, he or she is performing at an exceptional level of effectiveness.

Perform at Your Best

Immediately after you have made a sale, you like yourself more as a salesperson. You feel more confident, competent, and effective in selling. If you have been working on a difficult prospect and you have just closed a sale, get in your car and drive straight over to that tough customer and attempt to make the sale. You will be amazed at how many times this turns out to be an effective strategy. You will be more persuasive right after having made a sale than at any other time.

It will not be the customer who has changed. It won't be the product or service, or the price, the market, or the competition. The only thing that has changed is *you.*

Nothing Will Stop You

One of the things we know in sales is that "success breeds success." The more you sell, the better you become at selling. Your self-concept as a salesperson gets better and better. You finally reach the point in your own thinking where you know that nothing can stop you. If you continue to sell long enough, you will begin to have repeated success experiences. As you sell more and more, your self-concept improves to the point at which you become convinced that you are an excellent salesperson, and that you can make a great living in sales wherever you go.

When you are feeling terrific about yourself, when you really like yourself, you know that you can do well in anything that you put your hand to. When you are selling well, your family and interpersonal relationships seem to be much better. You need less sleep. You have more energy. You have more enthusiasm. You feel more positive about yourself.

The Power of Positive Affirmations

The key to reaching this state of mind is to prepare yourself psychologically before every sales call. Stop and take a couple of seconds; then say to yourself, "I like myself! I like myself! I like myself!"

Talking to yourself positively is like pumping yourself up. Just like pumping up a tire, you pump up your self-esteem. First thing in the morning when you get out of bed, start talking to yourself by saying, "I like myself, and I love my work! I like myself, and I love my work!"

Whatever you say to yourself with feeling is accepted by your subconscious as an instruction, a command. Your subconscious mind will then give you the words, actions, and feelings consistent with the message that you have sent to it.

Before going in to see a prospect, say to yourself, "I am a great salesperson, and this is going to be a great call!" Repeat that several times. Get yourself psychologically prepared for a good experience.

When you then walk in to see the prospect, your subconscious will give you the words, the feelings, and the body language consistent with a person who is excellent at what he does. Talking to yourself positively makes you more confident. It causes you to relax and perform better. Your level of self-confidence and calmness has a strong impact on the person you are talking to. Positive self-talk leads to positive sales results.

Obstacles to Sales Success

There are two major obstacles to making and closing any sale. They are both mental. They are the *fear of failure* and the *fear of rejection.*

The fear of failure is the biggest single reason for failure in adult life. It is not failure itself, but the fear of failure, the prospect of failure, the anticipation of failure, that causes you to freeze up and perform at a lower level.

The fear of failure is a deep subconscious fear that we all develop early in life, usually as the result of destructive criticism from one or both parents when we are children. If your parents criticized you continually when you were growing up, you will experience this deeply entrenched, unconscious fear of failure as an adult, at least until you learn to get rid of it.

Why Customers Don't Buy

The fear of failure in the mind of the customer or the prospect is the one greatest obstacle to buying. Every customer has made countless buying mistakes. He has purchased services that he later found were overpriced. He has bought products that broke down and that he could not get repaired. He has been sold things that he did not want, could not use, and could not afford. He has been burned so many times in sales experiences that he is like a long-tailed cat in a room full of rocking chairs.

This fear of failure and disappointment is the number one reason why customers do not buy. So, one of the most important things you can do in the process of building trust and credibility is to reduce the customer's fear to the point where he has no hesitation about going ahead with your offer.

The Fear of Rejection

The second major obstacle to selling and closing is the *fear of rejection*. This is the fear that the potential buyer might say no. The fear of rejection is triggered by the possibility of rudeness, disapproval, or criticism toward the salesperson by the prospect.

The rule is that 80 percent of sales calls will end in a no, for a thousand different reasons. This does not necessarily mean that there is anything wrong with the salesperson or the product or service being sold. People say no because they simply do not need it, do not want it, cannot use it, cannot afford it, or some other reason.

If you are in sales and you fear rejection, you've picked the wrong way to make a living.

If you are in sales and you fear rejection, you've picked the wrong way to make a living. The fact is that you are going to get a lot of rejections. As they say, "It goes with the territory."

Every experience of failure or rejection affects your self-esteem. It hurts your self-image. It makes you feel bad about yourself and triggers your worst fear: "I'm not good enough."

If it were not for the fear of rejection, we would all be terrific salespeople. We would all make twice as much, and maybe even five or ten times as much.

The Salesperson's Average Day

In a study at Columbia University a few years ago, they found that the average salesperson works approximately one and a half hours per day. They also found that, on the average, the first sales call is not made before eleven o'clock in the morning. The final sales call is usually made at about three thirty in the afternoon, and the average salesperson quits working shortly after that. He goes back to the office or heads for home.

Most people spend half the morning getting warmed up, drinking coffee, chatting with coworkers, reading the paper, shuffling their business cards, and surfing the Internet. Then they go out and make a sales call just in time for lunch. The second sales call isn't made until about 1:00 or 2:00 PM, after which the average salesperson begins winding down for the day. The total amount of time spent face-to-face with customers works out to about ninety minutes per day. That is the average—half are above; half are below that average.

The Brake on Sales Performance

Why is it that salespeople work so little and avoid getting face-to-face with customers so much? Simple: fear of rejection. The fear of rejection acts like a subconscious "brake" that holds people back and causes them to underperform. Of course, they always have a wonderful selection of excuses and rationalizations, but the real reason is fear of rejection.

It is easy to prove this. Let us conduct an experiment. Imagine that your company has hired a marketing research firm to find customers for you. This firm has developed a sophisticated way of identifying ideal prospects. Using this system, they can give you a computer print-out of fifty prospects that will be literally guaranteed, with 90 percent accuracy, to buy on a particular day. This list of hot, qualified prospects is so precise that it is only valid for twenty-four hours. Imagine that they call you in and give you this list of fifty top prospects for the following day.

If you received a list of fifty highly qualified prospects, 90 percent of whom were guaranteed to buy if you could call on them within that one-day period, what time would you start in the morning? How much time would you take for coffee breaks or lunch during the day? How long would you spend chatting with your colleagues and reading the newspaper? If you were guaranteed a sale to virtually every single person you spoke to in a one-day period, you would probably start at the crack of dawn and keep on going until midnight if you possibly could. If you had no fear of rejection and you were guaranteed a high level of success, you would be calling on prospects every single waking moment.

Rejection Is Not Personal

All top salespeople have reached the point where they no longer fear rejection. They have built their self-esteem and self-concepts up such that if someone says no to them, it does not hurt them or put them off. It does not send them dejected back to their offices or cars.

Here's the key to dealing with rejection. You must realize that rejection is not personal. It is not aimed at you. Rejection has nothing to do with you. Instead, it is like the rain or the sunshine. It just happens from day to day. When you can rise above yourself, stop taking yourself so seriously, and recognize that rejection simply goes with the territory, it will have no more fear for you. You will ignore it like water off a duck's back. You will expect it in the normal course of things, shrug your shoulders, and move on to the next prospect.

There is a sales motto: "Some will; some won't; so what? Next!" This should be your motto as well.

Never Give Up

Perhaps the two most fundamental qualities for success in sales are boldness and persistence. It takes courage to get up each day and constantly face the fears of failure and rejection. It takes persistence to keep coming back, day after day, in spite of continued difficulties and disappointment.

But the good news is that courage is a habit. Like a muscle, the more you practice courage, the stronger you become. Eventually, you reach the point at which you are virtually unafraid. After that, your career takes off like a rocket.

Five Calls or Closes

A full 80 percent of sales are never closed before the fifth meeting or closing attempt. It is after the fifth time that you ask the prospect to make a buying decision that you make most of your sales.

These numbers turn out to be valid especially when you are trying to get your prospect to change from buying from one company to buying from your company. At least eight out of ten of all first purchases from a new supplier take place after the fifth call or visit.

It seems that only about 10 percent of salespeople make more than five calls or attempts to close the sale. Half of all salespeople, or more, make only one call before they give up. When you are selling to a company that you want to switch from their existing supplier to you, remember that it usually takes about five visits to break down the prospect's natural skepticism and resistance.

This does not mean that you have to spend five hours. It just means that you have to make five visits or more. You have to make an appointment, go and see the prospect, talk to him, tell him that you and your

company are available to serve him. It is usually after the fifth visit that
the prospect starts to become interested.

Most People Quit Early

In a recent study, it was discovered that 48 percent of all sales calls
end without the salesperson trying to close even *once*. The salesperson
meets with the prospect, talks enthusiastically about his product or service, shows him the written information, and dazzles him with reasons to
buy. Then, when the prospect has been completely overwhelmed with his
charm, enthusiasm, and verbal agility, he takes a deep breath, sits back,
and says, "Well, what do you think?"

This almost automatically triggers the response, "Well, I'd like to
think it over." The prospect says he wants to talk it over with his boss, wife,
cousin, brother, uncle, sister, partner, board of directors, banker, accountant, and whoever else he can think of. "Could you call me back later?"

Prospects Don't Think It Over

One of the important secrets of success in sales is for you to understand and accept that people don't "think it over." The minute you walk
out of the prospect's office or home, he or she forgets that you ever lived.

Have you ever gone back to see a prospect a week later, after you
thought you had a fantastic sales conversation and he was thinking it over?
Some salespeople have the vanity to believe that this prospect has gone
home and has been thinking about their product or service twenty-four
hours a day. They think he turns it over in his mind and talks about it with
everyone he meets. He thinks about it and dreams about it, just waiting
for you to come back.

Then, when you visit the prospect a week or two later, you are amazed
to find that he has forgotten your name, your product, and everything
else. He doesn't remember who you are or what you sell. He has not been
thinking about you *or* your product or service at all.

People don't think things over with regard to products or sales. These words are a polite way of saying, "Good-bye forever." When they say to you, "Let me think it over," they are announcing to you that the interview is over and that you have lost your entire investment of time and energy in this prospect.

Self-Esteem Eliminates Fear

The reason I mention this direct relationship between courage and persistence on the one hand, and making multiple calls and sales success on the other, is this: there is a direct and inverse relationship between the fears of rejection and failure, and high self-esteem. The more you like yourself, the less you feel rejection and the less you fear failure.

Imagine two escalators that go in different directions. One is the up escalator to high self-esteem, and the other is the down escalator to the fears of failure and rejection that hold you back. The more you like your-self and the higher your self-esteem, the faster you go up the escalator to courage and confidence. The more you think about failure or rejection, the more you ride the down escalator toward fears of failure and rejection.

You Are a Good Person

When a person says no to you, he is not saying no to you *as a person*. He is simply saying no to your offering or your presentation or your prices. The rejection is not personal. Once you know and understand that saying no is not personal, you stop worrying about it when people react to you or your product negatively.

Here's the danger: if you take a "no" personally, you can start to think there is something wrong with you as an individual. Or you begin to believe that your product or your company is faulty. When you begin thinking like this, you can soon become discouraged. You will lose your enthusiasm for selling. As a result, you will start cutting back on prospect-ing. Soon you will only be working an hour and a half per day.

Fear Leads to Excuses for Not Selling

As your fears increase, you will begin to rationalize and justify your nonselling behavior. You will make excuses and create all kinds of "make-work" at the office. You will convince yourself that you have to read the newspaper so that you will be fully informed when you call on prospects. You have to shuffle your business cards and check the office to see if there have been any phone calls. You have all those people out there who are "thinking it over." Maybe one of them has called and ordered something.

You go into the office and plan your first hour or two around a couple of cups of coffee. After all, you have to wake yourself up in the morning so that you are sharp and alert when you go out to see customers. You chat with your coworkers and talk about business, especially how tough the business is. You kill most of the morning; then you realize that you had better go out and call on somebody, anybody. So you rush out and make a call just before it's time for lunch.

An Unproductive Day

You wouldn't want to interrupt prospects when they are going for lunch. Therefore, you don't make any calls after 11:30 AM. You go and have lunch with your friends, go shopping, get your car washed, or kill time.

Time passes. You certainly don't want to call on people immediately after they get back from lunch. It might disturb their digestion. So you make up a few more excuses and rationalizations, and you don't make your next call until 2:00 or 3:00 PM. Soon it's 3:30, then 4:00, and of course, everybody's on their way home, aren't they?

You don't want to go out and bother people late in the afternoon while they are preparing to wrap up for the day. Instead, you go back to the office to commiserate with the other salespeople who are gathering there like survivors after an accident and talk about what a tough day you've had.

There is the story of the two salesmen who go back to the office at the end of the day. One says, "Boy, did I ever have a lot of good interviews today!"

The other one says, "Yeah, I didn't sell anything either."

Can you identify with any of these behaviors? They are the favorite practices and excuses of salespeople in the bottom 20 percent of money earners in their fields.

Increase Traveling Time

Another way that salespeople avoid the possibility of failure and rejection is by spreading out their sales calls geographically. Such a salesperson makes one call at one end of town and makes her second call in the afternoon at the other end of town. This gives her a nice solid hour of driving in between, which allows her to pretend that she is working, when in reality, she is just putting off getting face-to-face with a prospect.

The fears of failure and rejection, which lower your self-esteem, quickly become the major obstacles to success in sales.

Build Your Self-Esteem, Increase Your Income

Everything you do to raise your own self-esteem, including positive self-talk, affirmative visualization, personal motivation, enthusiasm, and individual training improves your personality and increases your effectiveness in selling.

As we said before, there is a direct relationship between your self-esteem and how much money you earn. The more you like yourself, the more sales you make and the higher your income will be. When you organize your life so that you become a perpetual self-esteem-generating person, that alone will contribute more to your income than any other factor.

The Friendship Factor

Customers today are spoiled. They are demanding. They are disloyal. They insist on being treated extremely well before they buy anything.

More than anything else, customers will only buy from people they like. We call this the "friendship factor."

The friendship factor in selling simply says that a prospect will not buy from you until he is genuinely convinced that you are his friend and that you are acting in his best interests.

For this reason, the first thing you do in a sales interview is create a bond, make a friend. Sales expert Heinz Goldman once wrote a book with a title that summarized this process perfectly: *How to Win Customers.* Your job as a sales professional is to win people over to your side by making it clear that you care about them and want the best for them.

Build a Bridge

You can only begin selling after you have convinced the prospect that you are his pal and that you want what is best for him. In fact, if you begin talking about your product or service before you have built a bridge of friendship to your prospect, the customer will lose all interest in buying from you. If you don't genuinely care about the customer, why should the customer care about you or what you are offering?

Healthy Personality

An excellent definition of a healthy personality is this: "Your personality is healthy to the degree to which you can get along with the greatest number of different types of people." You have an *un*healthy or problem personality to the degree to which you can*not* get along with most other people. People at the highest level of healthy personality have developed the ability to get along with the greatest variety of different people, especially in selling. The point is, the level of your self-esteem corresponds directly with the health of your personality. Again, the more you like yourself, the more you enjoy others and the more they like you. The more you like yourself, the easier it is for you to get along with a great variety of people.

Making Friends

The individual with high self-esteem is the one who has the greatest facility for making friends wherever he goes. Because he likes himself, he is naturally and spontaneously fond of others. When people feel that someone genuinely likes them, they are more open to listening to that person and to buying what he is selling.

> **When people feel that someone genuinely likes them, they are more open to listening to that person and to buying what he is selling.**

Have you ever had an experience where you wanted to buy a product or service, but you didn't like the salesperson? In most cases you will walk away, even if the product and the price are ideal.

Think of your very best customers today. The people you enjoy selling to and the people who enjoy buying from you are invariably the people that you like the most and who like you in return.

Your Self-Esteem Determines Your Income

Everything you do to improve your level of self-esteem increases and enhances the quality of your relationships with your customers. Self-esteem building actions trigger the "friendship factor" and make you a more successful salesperson. Your level of self-esteem in selling determines the amount of money that you earn. The very best salespeople have a natural capacity to make friends easily with prospective customers.

Unfortunately, everything that happens to lower your self-esteem will lower your sales effectiveness as well. If you are tired or unwell for any reason, your effectiveness will decrease. If you have arguments with your boss or your spouse, this will lower your self-esteem, sometimes to the point at which you can't sell anything at all.

The Catalyst for Sales Success

The primary emotion in sales success is *enthusiasm.* Enthusiasm accounts for 50 percent or more of all sales ability. One of the very best definitions of a sale is "a transfer of enthusiasm."

When you transfer your enthusiasm for your product or service into the mind and heart of your prospect, like an electrical connection, the sale takes place. When your emotional commitment and belief in the goodness of what you are selling transfers into the mind of the prospect or customer, all hesitation to buy disappears.

Once again, there is a direct link between how much you like yourself, your self-esteem, and your level of enthusiasm. The more you like yourself, the more enthusiastic you are. The more enthusiastic you are about your company and your product, the more enthusiastic the customer will become. Anything you do to raise your self-esteem will *increase* your ability to sell.

Emotions Are Contagious

In the inner game of selling, it is essential that you understand that *emotions are contagious.* Each person is affected by the emotions of other people. When you are positive, confident, and enthusiastic about your goods or service, the prospect picks up these emotions from you and becomes positive and enthusiastic as well.

Here's the key: You cannot give away something that you don't already have. You cannot convey enthusiasm if you don't have it yourself. This is why top salespeople love their merchandise or service and love the field of selling. Their enthusiasm is heartfelt and genuine. Prospects pick it up at an unconscious level and want to participate in whatever is making them feel so good about themselves and their work. Because of their confidence and passion, prospects want to buy from them and recommend them to their friends.

Failure Is Not an Option

It is critical that you back your sales efforts with *willpower* and *determination*. Decide now that you will *not give up*.

When you resolve in advance that you will never give up, you will be mentally prepared to bounce back from failure and rejection. When you continue to persist, no matter how difficult the situation, you will eventually succeed. You will ultimately make sales. You will finally win customers.

Whenever you make a sale, you feel like a "winner." Each time you close, your self-esteem goes up and your self-concept improves. Your self-image is reinforced.

The more you like yourself, the better you will do in sales, and in every other part of your life. Your ability to perform and your level of effectiveness increase in your nonbusiness activities.

The reason so many people fail in sales is simply because they do not persist long enough and work hard enough to get those first few winning experiences. Once you begin to make sales and feel like a winner, you become even more motivated to sell *even more* of your product or service. But if you don't have those first successful experiences, you can easily lose heart and begin thinking that selling is not for you.

Practice Mental Rehearsal

Mental rehearsal is vital. The more you preprogram yourself to bounce back, the easier it is for you to overcome the failures and rejections that are part of the selling life. Talk to yourself positively. Say things like "I can do it! I can do it! I can do it!" whenever you feel fears of failure or rejection.

Interestingly enough, when you make the decision that no matter what happens, you will never give up, your self-esteem increases immediately. You respect yourself more. Your self-confidence skyrockets. Even though you have not yet stepped out of your office, the very act of making the decision that you are going to succeed, that you can do it, that you will never quit, no matter what, improves your "reputation" with yourself. You *see* yourself in a more positive light. You feel more like a winner. You are more composed and self-assured. You become more capable of dealing with the ups and downs of daily selling life. The very act of resolving to persist until you succeed changes your personality and makes you a stronger and more powerful person.

ACTION EXERCISES

1. Decide today to become a totally confident, high-self-esteem salesperson; say over and over to yourself, "I like myself!"

2. Visualize yourself continually as the very best in your business; the person you "see" is the person you will "be."

3. Resolve in advance that, no matter what happens, you will never give up; failure is not an option.

4. Refuse to take rejection personally; accept it as a normal and natural part of selling, very much like the weather.

5. Follow the leaders in your field; pattern yourself after the highest-paid and most successful people. Find out what they are doing, and then do the same things until you get the same results.

6. Make a decision today to join the top 20 percent of people in your business; remember that no one is smarter than you, and no one is better than you. Anything that anyone else has done, within reason, you can do as well.

7. Take action on every new idea that you think can help you in any way. Give it a try. The more things you try, the more likely it is that you will eventually triumph.

We advance on our journey only when we face our goal,
only when we are confident and believe we are going to win out.
—ORISON SWETT MARDEN

2

SET AND ACHIEVE
ALL YOUR SALES GOALS

*If I've got correct goals, and I keep pursuing them the best
way I know how, everything else falls into line. If I do the
right thing, I know I'm going to succeed.*
—DAN DIERDORF

Top salespeople are intensely goal oriented. In every study, the quality of *goal orientation* seems to be associated with high levels of success and achievement. The highest-paid salespeople know in advance how much they are going to earn each week, each month, each quarter, and each year. They know how many calls they will have to make to achieve a particular level of sales, and they have clear plans about what they are going to do with the money they earn.

It is essential for your success that you decide exactly how much you intend to earn each year. If you are not absolutely clear about your earnings target, your sales activities will be unfocused. You will be like a person trying to shoot at a target in the fog. Even if you are the finest marksman in the world, you are not going to hit a target you can't see. You have to know exactly what you're aiming at.

Your Annual Income Goal

Begin with your annual income goal. How much do you intend to make in the next twelve months? What is the exact number? Write this number down. This becomes the target toward which you orient all of your activities throughout the year.

You need a goal that is realistic, but challenging. Take your highest income year to date and increase that amount by 25 to 50 percent, whatever amount you are comfortable with. Be sure to make your goal believable and achievable. Ridiculous goals do not motivate you; they demotivate you, because deep in your heart, you know that they are unattainable. As a result, you will quit at the first sign of adversity.

Top salespeople in every field know exactly what they are going to earn each year and each part of each year. If you ask them, they can tell you within a dollar what they are aiming at every single day.

Low-performing salespeople have no idea how much they are going to earn. They have to wait until the end of the year and get their tax forms to find out what happened. For them, every day, month, and year is a new financial adventure. They have no idea where they are going to end up.

Put Them in Writing

To be effective, your goals must be in writing. Sometimes people are reluctant to write their goals down on paper. They say, "What if I don't make it?" You don't need to worry. The very act of writing your goals down increases your likelihood of achieving them by 1,000 percent—ten times—and usually far faster then you expected.

Even if you don't hit your goal on schedule, it is still better for you to have a written goal than to have no goal at all.

Your Annual Sales Goal

The second part of goal setting is for you to ask yourself, "How much am I going to have to sell this year to achieve my personal income goal?"

This should not be too difficult to calculate. Even if you work on a combination of base plus commission, you should be able to determine the exact sales volume required for you to earn the amount of money that you want.

Monthly and Weekly Goals

Once you have decided your annual income and sales goals, break them down *by month*. How much will you have to earn and sell each month to achieve your annual goals?

Once you have your annual sales and income goals and your monthly sales and income goals, break them down to *weekly* sales and income goals. How much will you have to sell each week in order to achieve your long-term goals?

Daily Sales Goals

Finally, determine how much you have to *sell* each day to earn the amount you want to *earn* each day.

Let us say that your annual income goal is $50,000. If you divide $50,000 by 12, you get approximately $4,200 per month. If you divide $50,000 by 50, the number of weeks that you work in an average year, it comes out to $1,000 per week. Now you have definite, specific targets to aim at.

Set Clear Activity Goals

The final step in setting sales goals is for you to determine the specific *activities* in which you must engage to achieve your desired sales level. How many *calls* will you have to make to get how many *appointments* with prospects? How many presentations and callbacks will you have to generate to achieve a specific level of sales?

When you keep accurate records day by day and month by month, you will soon be able to predict with considerable accuracy exactly what you will have to do each day and each week to achieve your monthly and annual income goals.

Let us assume that you will have to make ten prospecting calls a day to get sufficient appointments to make enough sales to achieve your goals. Make it a game with yourself to make your ten prospecting calls before noon each day. Set this as your daily activity target, and then discipline yourself to follow through on your plan.

Get on the phone by eight or eight thirty in the morning, or get out and cold-call, if you have to. Whatever you do, force yourself to make your ten calls before noon, every single day, until it becomes a habit.

You Control Your Sales Life

The most important part of planning your activities is knowing that sales activities *are controllable.* You cannot decide or determine where a particular sale will come from. But you can control the *inputs,* the activities that you must engage in to achieve the sales in the first place. And by controlling your activities, you indirectly control your sales results.

Some days and weeks will be better than others. Sometimes you will make a lot of sales, and sometimes you won't make any. Sometimes you will have dry periods and sales slumps. Other times you will sell two or three times as much as you projected. But the law of averages is at work. It is inexorable. If you just keep on making the necessary calls, you will eventually make your sales, on schedule.

Your Results May Amaze You

In many cases, when you start setting goals for the week, month, and year, and start working toward them systematically each day, you will hit those goals far *faster* than you expected. Many of my students set one-year goals and hit them in six or seven months. Some people have actually hit their sales goals for the entire year in as little as three months.

Whenever you start setting clear, specific goals for every part of your

sales life, you will be amazed at the results. Some of my seminar participants have worked for years selling a particular product in a specific market. But they had never set goals before. The first year after they began
setting goals, their sales exploded. They suddenly started breaking sales
records, even though they were still selling the same product out of the
same office, to the same people at the same prices. Goal setting made the
difference.

Tap Into Your Subconscious Mind

This happens because the very act of *writing* a goal programs it into
your subconscious mind. Once you have programmed a goal into your
subconscious mind, it takes on a power of its own. Your subconscious
mind works twenty-four hours per day, sleeping and waking, and starts
guiding you rapidly toward the achievement of this goal.

> **Once you have programmed a goal into your subcon-
> scious mind, it takes on a power of its own.**

Your subconscious alerts you to opportunities and possibilities around
you. It brings you the right ideas for the right things to say, sometimes
in the middle of a sales conversation. Once you program a goal into your
subconscious mind, it continually motivates you into taking the actions
necessary to achieve it.

Sometimes, your subconscious mind will help you read your
prospect's face, giving you a better sense of what to say. Everyone has experienced being in a sales presentation where he simply couldn't make a mistake or say the wrong word. The sales presentation went smoothly from
beginning to end and concluded with a closed sale. Whenever this happens, it is because your mind is perfectly programmed, at a subconscious
level, to enable you to perform at your best in the pursuit of your goals.

The Right Words at the Right Time

When you feel excellent about yourself, your subconscious mind will give you exactly the right words at exactly the right time. It will make you sensitive to physical cues and verbal clues that will guide you to bring up a subject that you hadn't even thought about. But it will turn out, from the customer's point of view, to be exactly the right thing to say.

You might mention that your company has an excellent reputation for customer service and after-sales follow-up. You later learn that this was the prospect's primary concern and was exactly what he needed to hear to buy from you.

As previously stated, the average person uses only 10 percent of his potential. By programming your subconscious mind with clear goals, you gain access to the 90 percent of your potential that lies beneath the surface, deep in your subconscious mind. You program your subconscious and access it on a regular basis by deciding exactly how much you want to earn and precisely what activities you will have to undertake to earn that amount of money.

Set Personal and Family Goals

You also need personal and family goals. These are the reasons *why* you do what you do. These are the reasons that you get up in the morning and work all day, in the face of disappointments and difficulties. The greater clarity you have with regard to your family and personal goals, the more motivated you will be and the faster you will bounce back from temporary failure and rejection.

Imagine that you could *double* your income in the next two or three years. If you did, what are some of the things you would change in your life? Make a list of all the things that you would *be, have,* or *do* if you were earning vastly more money than you are earning today. The longer this list, the greater your level of motivation and determination.

Build a Fire Under Your Desire

If you have only one or two reasons for achieving your financial goals, you will be easily discouraged by setbacks and difficulties. If you have ten or fifteen reasons for being successful, you will be more motivated and determined. But if you have fifty or one hundred reasons for increasing your sales and your income, you will become virtually unstoppable.

When it comes to aggressively selling your product or service, who do you think will be *more* motivated? Will it be the person with one or two reasons to succeed, or the person with fifty-plus reasons? The fact is that the more reasons you have, the greater will be the intensity of your desire, like a roaring furnace. The more you want it, the more guaranteed it is that you will do *whatever it takes* to achieve it. The more reasons you give yourself, the more of your subconscious powers will be available to you in each selling situation.

Set 100 Goals

Here is an exercise for you. Get a spiral notebook and write down 100 goals that you would like to accomplish in the years ahead. Make a list of everything that you would like to have in your life and everything that you would like to do. Imagine that everything you write on this list is going to come to you at exactly the right time and in exactly the right way. You only have to write it down, as if submitting an order to the great cosmic storehouse of wealth, in order to get it. As you think of new things that you would like to have or accomplish, write them in this spiral notebook. You can never have too many goals.

A friend of mine who was just starting in sales began this exercise by writing down more than 350 goals for himself for the years ahead. Every time he read the newspaper or watched television and saw something that he wanted, he wrote it in his spiral notebook. Every week, he read and reviewed his goals and added new ones.

Within one year, in a competitive market, from a dead start, he became one of the most successful salespeople in his field. He eventually broke every sales record in his industry. He was written up in the newspapers as a "sales superstar."

He told me privately that writing and reviewing his goals was the primary reason for the motivation and enthusiasm that led to his success. He eventually came to feel that he was unstoppable.

The Number One Reason for Success

In my work with more than 500,000 salespeople throughout the United States and in twenty-five countries, I have found that the commitment to goal setting has been the number one reason for the success of the top people. All the highest-paid sales professionals in every field are committed goal setters. They write and rewrite their goals every day. They continually add to their lists. They access and activate their subconscious and superconscious minds. They begin to attract into their lives people and circumstances that help them achieve their goals.

Visualize Your Goals as Realized

When used with goal setting, *visualization* is perhaps the most powerful skill that you can develop. There is no more powerful way to program your subconscious mind than to create a clear mental picture of the person you want to be and the goals you want to accomplish.

The power of visualization is the most awesome power possessed by human beings. It is said that all improvement in your life begins with an improvement in your mental pictures. When you visualize, see yourself as calm, confident, and powerful. Envision yourself as successful and influential. Picture yourself as capable and competent in every part of selling. See yourself as absolutely excellent in prospecting, presenting, and closing sales.

Before you go into a sales meeting, imagine the prospect responding to you in a positive, enthusiastic way. See him or her smiling and engaged in the sales conversation. Picture especially the prospect signing the sales order or writing out the check. You will be amazed at how often your visualization will turn into reality when you are with the customer.

Say It and See It

Your subconscious mind is activated both by pictures and by strong affirmative statements. Each time you say something strongly to yourself, your subconscious mind accepts these words as a command. It then goes to work to bring that command into your reality.

The very best all-purpose affirmation is "I like myself! I like myself! I like myself!" As I have already shown, each time you say "I like myself!" you raise your self-esteem, improve your overall self-concept, and perform more effectively in whatever you are doing, especially in sales.

When you repeat an affirmation as a command to your subconscious mind with confidence and enthusiasm, you activate all your mental powers. You increase your energy levels. You feel more positive and enthusiastic. You take complete control over your mind and emotions.

Say to yourself, "I feel happy. I feel healthy. I feel terrific!" Repeat this over and over again as you go through your day. Every time you repeat these words, you will feel happier and more confident. Then *see* yourself as if you felt this way.

From the Bottom to the Top

At a seminar recently a sales manager told me a story. She said her company had hired a young salesman with limited experience. They were not sure whether he would be successful, but they decided to give him a chance. Within six months however, he was the top salesman in the entire country for that company. They sat him down and asked him why he felt he was doing so well, considering that he had never worked in this industry before. How was he outperforming and outselling professional salespeople who had been in the industry for ten or fifteen years?

His secret? He was using affirmations and visualization *every day*. He said, "Every morning when I get into my car, I repeat to myself, 'I'm the best! I'm the best! I'm the best.'

"I then say, 'I'm the best salesman in this company. I'm the best salesman in this industry. I'm the best salesman in the business.'

"Before every sales call, I sit in my car and pump myself up by repeating these affirmations, 'I'm the best in this company. I'm the best in this industry. I'm the best in this country.'"

Create a Clear Mental Picture

This inspiring salesman went on to explain that while he was talking to himself positively, he would create a clear mental picture of himself selling and interacting with the customer exactly as if he was the top salesman in the nation. He imagined the prospect responding to him positively and confidently. He would relax, smile, and enjoy the feeling that he anticipates having when he gets face-to-face with a customer.

When he went in to see the prospect, he radiated confidence. He was warm, friendly, and self-assured. He was courteous and respectful. He created instant rapport with everyone in the company, especially the customer. And customers bought from him in record numbers.

Choose Your Words and Pictures

Here is an interesting discovery. *Everyone* visualizes and talks to themselves continually as they go about their daily business. The difference between top salespeople and average salespeople is the *content* of their inner dialogue and their mental pictures. Top salespeople think and talk about their best selling experiences in the past. They then imagine that they are going to repeat those *excellent* experiences in the upcoming sales call.

Mediocre salespeople visualize and affirm as well. Unfortunately, they think about their most recent *negative* experiences. They think about wasted time and energy on people who didn't buy, customers who were rude or indifferent, and how disappointed they felt.

In either case, by visualizing and affirming, the salesperson is setting himself up mentally to *repeat* the previous experience. When you create a positive, exciting picture of your very best previous sales experience, your subconscious mind projects that experience, like a picture on a screen, onto your next sales call. With this clear picture, your subconscious orchestrates your thoughts, feelings, and actions so that you do and say the same things that you did and said before to be so successful.

You Control Your Subconscious Mind

Your subconscious mind is neutral. It is like clay. You can shape it any way you want. Your subconscious does not think or decide. It merely *obeys* your mental commands. When you take full control of your conscious mind and discipline yourself to think and talk about only the things you want, you send clear commands to your subconscious mind to give you the thoughts, words, and actions that will make you successful.

Selling Like Columbus

Many salespeople are what we call "Columbus salespeople." When Columbus set off seeking a route to India, he didn't know where he was *going*. When he arrived in the Americas, he didn't know where he *was*. And when he got back to Spain, he didn't know where he had *been*.

Many salespeople are like this. They set off in the morning with only a vague idea of where they are going. When they arrive at the customer's home or place of business, they say the first thing that falls out of their mouths. And when they arrive back at the office, they are not sure where they have been or what happened.

Plan Your Calls In Advance

Top salespeople are different. They think through their sales calls in advance. They go over what they are going to say mentally before they get face-to-face with the prospect. They practice "mental rehearsal," a peak-performance technique used by all top athletes, including sales athletes. They prepare mentally for the upcoming meeting.

If you were an athlete going into competition, you would never think of arriving at the field or court and then walking straight in to the competition. A professional athlete always warms up before going onto the field. By the same token, professional salespeople warm up as well by mentally rehearsing so that they can perform at their very best when they get face-to-face with their customer.

Two Ways to Visualize

There are two ways that you can use visualization to mentally rehearse your upcoming sales performance. The first is *direct*, whereby you "see" the customer and the sales situation through your own eyes. You see the customer smiling and responding to you in a positive way. You see him or her agreeing with you and enjoying your company and the sales presentation. This is very effective.

The second way you can use visualization is *indirectly*. With this method, you actually stand outside of yourself and see yourself and the customer in the sales situation, exactly as if you were a third party watching from the side. When you use both of these methods alternately, seeing yourself from both the inside and the outside, you dramatically improve the quality of your sales presentation and personal performance.

See Yourself as the Best

Continually imagine yourself as the very best in your field. See yourself as one of the highest money earners in your business. Model yourself after the highest-paid salespeople in your industry. Walk, talk, and treat others as if you were already a sales superstar.

When you see someone else driving a new car or dressed in expensive clothes and wearing an expensive watch, say to yourself, "That's for me!"

You decide that whatever anyone else has accomplished, you can achieve as well. There are no limits.

ACTION
EXERCISES

1. Think big! Set an income goal for yourself for the next year that is 25 to 50 percent more than you have ever earned before.

2. Determine how much of your product or service you will have to sell over the next year to achieve your ideal income.

3. Break your income and sales goals down by month, week, and day; determine the activities you will have to engage in each day to earn the money you have decided that you desire.

4. Plan every day in advance; determine exactly the number of prospects you will have to call, the number of people you will have to see, and the number of sales you will have to make.

5. Set big, exciting goals for your family and your personal life; make a list of fifty to one hundred things that you want to buy and do with the extra money you are going to earn.

6. Make a written plan to achieve each of your goals, and work on your plans every day.

7. Determine the price you will have to pay, in terms of additional work and sacrifice, to achieve your most desired goals, and then begin paying that price.

You too can determine what you want. You can decide on your major objectives, targets, aims and destinations.

—W. CLEMENT STONE

*You cannot teach a man anything; you can only help him
discover it within himself.*
—GALILEO GALILEI

There are many different reasons why someone may buy your product or service. What you must appreciate is that people buy for *their* reasons, not for yours. One of the biggest mistakes amateur salespeople make is asking people to buy for their own personal reasons, not for the reasons that actually motivate the customer to take action.

One of the most significant parts of selling, the indispensable step upon which the whole sales process depends, is your ability to identify the needs of your prospect accurately. You must take whatever time is necessary and ask as many questions as possible to find out exactly why this particular prospect needs to buy your product or service at this time. If you fail to identify the prospect's needs accurately, the entire sales process will grind to a halt.

The Basic Motivation

As a fundamental principle, every human action is aimed at an *improvement* of some kind. People buy products and services because they feel they will be better off as a result. They not only feel that they will be better off as a result of buying your product or service, but they also feel they will be better off than if they bought some *other* product or service, or if they bought nothing at all.

Every customer has three choices with every selling offer. He can buy from you, buy from someone else, or buy nothing at all at this time. Your job is to get the customer to understand that he needs your product enough to overcome any buying resistance that might derail the sale.

In addition, the customer must be *substantially* better off with your product or service than he is without it. It cannot represent a *small* increment in value or benefit. The improvement in the prospect's work or life must be great enough to justify the amount of money you are charging, plus the amount of time and energy it will take to implement your solution.

The Greatest Value

People value *freedom* above almost all other benefits of our society. When they have money available, they have a certain degree of freedom. They have choices and options. They can do a variety of different things. This desire for freedom is a major reason people hesitate to part with their money, for any reason.

If a prospect buys from you, he gives up a certain amount of the flexibility and freedom that he had before giving you the money. If he buys a product from you that is unsatisfactory, he no longer has the money and is *stuck* with the product. Since every prospect has had this experience more than once, there is always a certain amount of buying resistance.

The More, the Better

Economists talk about "units of satisfaction." They postulate that different actions can give a person different degrees of satisfaction. The prospect wants to get as many of these units of satisfaction as possible in every purchase decision. He wants to be better off physically, emotionally, and even spiritually. He wants to be satisfied in a variety of ways.

The more diverse the ways that your product or service can please and satisfy your prospect, the easier it is for him to buy.

Emotional Values

Each person has different buying motivations. One of the most critical areas of sales psychology has to do with what are called "psychic" or "emotional" values. These are invisible, intangible values that attach to a product or service that make it appear and feel more valuable from the customer's perspective.

For example, often salespeople will try to convince the customer to buy by assuring him that their product or service is being sold at the very *best price* available in the market.

But frequently the prospect is more concerned about the name or reputation of the company selling the product. He would rather buy something that is better known, even if it costs more money.

If this is what is most important to the prospect, when the salesperson emphasizes the lower cost of an unknown product or service, he is actually *hurting* his chances of making the sale.

How Others Feel

People are sensitive to other people in their work or home environment. Whenever someone considers making a purchase, he or she thinks about how *other people* may respond to that purchase decision. No one wants to be criticized. If there is a chance that the prospect will be criticized by his boss or spouse for making a particular purchase, he will refrain from making that purchase altogether.

Price and Quality

Most salespeople parrot the words *price* and *quality* as if they were reasons to buy anything. In today's competitive market, it is assumed that your product or service is well priced and of a sufficiently high quality, or it wouldn't be available in the first place. Telling the prospect that he should buy your product because of your "price and quality" is very similar to saying that he should buy your product or service because you will deliver it to him. It is not a reason to buy at all.

Identifying Needs

Professional selling begins with *needs analysis*. You are not really in a position to sell until you have asked enough questions and listened closely enough to the answers. This enables you to understand the most intense need of the prospect that your product or service can satisfy.

Once you have identified the customer's key needs and wants, you can then structure your presentation in such a way that you demonstrate overwhelmingly to the customer that he will have that need satisfied if he buys from you.

Does Versus Is

Perhaps the chief distinction in needs analysis is the difference between what your product "is" and what your product "does." Most salespeople are preoccupied with what their product is, how it is made, and the specific features that go into its design and production. As a result, these are the things they talk about when they are with a prospect.

But the prospect does not care what your product *is*. He only cares about what your product or service will *do* for him. Every customer's favorite radio station is WII-FM, "What's In It For Me?"

> **The prospect does not care what your product is. He only cares about what your product or service will do for him.**

Here is a simple way to determine what your product does for your customer. Imagine a pipeline. Into one end of the pipeline goes your product or service from sale to delivery to actual use by the customer. Out of the other end of the pipeline, dropping into a bucket, is what your product does to improve the life or work of the customer. Your job is to clearly identify what arrives in the customer's bucket as the result of his or her buying what you are selling.

Emotional Versus Practical Reasons

For example, some people sell life insurance by stressing its affordability relative to competitive policies, the size and reputation of the company, the ease of monthly payments, and the role that life insurance pays in financial planning. These are all important, but they are not the reason that a customer buys life insurance. He buys it chiefly for "peace of mind."

One of the top life insurance agents in the country told me that he has a very simple question that he uses when calling on new prospects. He asks, "Do you feel responsible for providing for your family if something were to happen to you?"

If the prospect does not say yes to this question immediately, he spends no further time trying to convince him of the importance of life insurance. He has found that if a person does not feel highly responsible for his family, he will be reluctant to take out insurance to provide for them in case of an accident.

By the same token, there are questions that you can ask to determine if the emotional need that your product satisfies is important enough to your customer for him to buy what you are selling if you can convince him that this need will be satisfied. Your choice of questions is often the key to identifying needs correctly.

The Two Major Motivations

The two major reasons that people buy or don't buy, respectively, are desire for gain and fear of loss. The desire for gain is obviously to be better off, for an improvement in conditions of some kind. Your first task is to help your prospect understand how much better his life or work would be with your product compared to the way it is now.

The second motivation is fear of loss. As we've discussed earlier, prospects are afraid of making a buying mistake, of getting stuck with something they don't want, don't need, can't use, and can't afford. Since this has happened to them so many times in the past, they are cautious about allowing it to happen again.

Here's an interesting discovery. Desire for gain has a motivational power of 1.0. But fear of loss has a negative motivational power of 2.5. In other words, the fear of loss is two and a half times more powerful than the desire for gain. People are much more motivated to buy if they feel they are going to lose something by *not* buying, than they are in anticipation of the benefits they will enjoy if they *do* buy.

Demonstrate Both

Of course, the best sales presentation shows the prospect how much better off he will be if he buys *and*, simultaneously, how much worse off he will be if he neglects to buy.

For example, in selling a car, you could show what a wonderful automobile it is, how beautiful it is, and how well it drives. If the prospect likes the car but is still hesitant, you could point out that this is the last one available for at least two months, or the last time this car will be sold at this low, low price. Often a prospect who was indecisive about buying will make an immediate purchase decision when confronted with the possibility that he won't be able to get it at its current price—or get it at all.

Are You Believable?

Believability is perhaps the single most crucial requirement in your sales presentation. No matter how convinced you are that your product or service will do what you say it will do, the customer will still be skeptical.

Your job is to raise your credibility to the point at which the customer will have no reluctance in going ahead.

Just imagine, if a prospect was absolutely *convinced* that he would be far better off as a result of purchasing your product, and was absolutely convinced that you would stand behind the product or service 100 percent, virtually nothing would stop him from buying. Increasing your credibility to this point is your main mission in the sales process. And this requires that you identify needs accurately.

Appealing to Customer Needs

Each customer has certain basic human needs that motivate him or her to take action, including buying action. You must identify the *most important* needs that your product or service can satisfy for each particular customer to whom you speak. You must then convince him overwhelmingly that this particular need will be fulfilled by your product or service better than by *anything else available* in the market at this time or at this price.

1. Money

Everyone wants to have more money. This is a basic need. "Money makes the world go around." Whenever you can link your product or service to making or saving money for the customer, you will have his total attention.

2. Security

Each person has a fundamental need for security. Most people feel that if they had enough money, they would be completely secure. So although money is hard and cold, the need for security is warm and personal.

According to a University of Chicago study, people buy because of the way they anticipate *feeling* as a result of owning and using your product or service. It is this sense of emotional anticipation that you must trigger if you want to make a sale. It is not the features or benefits of your product as much as it is the feeling of pleasure or fulfillment that the customer imagines he or she will enjoy by buying from you.

The need for security, whether financial, emotional or physical, for ourselves and for our families, is such a deep and powerful need that any appeal to greater security will arouse interest on the part of the prospect. Just as no one ever feels he has too much freedom, very few people ever feel that they have too much security. They always want more.

Security Products and Services.

Today there is a booming market for every kind of security service or device for Net servers and computers. Home security systems are a billion-dollar industry. Various forms of insurance to provide security against accidents or unexpected reversals sell in the hundreds of billions of dollars each year. Anytime you can show a customer that he or she can be safer and more secure as a result of owning your product or service, you can create buying desire.

3. Being Liked

Everyone wants to be liked by others. We need to feel accepted and respected by the people around us. We want to be admired by our friends, neighbors, and associates. Achieving these goals satisfies our deep need for belonging and self-worth.

How does your product or service increase the amount that your prospect is liked and respected by others?

4. Status and Prestige

One of the most powerful motivations for people is status or personal prestige. We want to feel and be perceived as important and valuable. We want people to look up to us and praise our possessions or accomplishments.

When you pay up to fifty dollars for a watch, you are buying a time-piece, something that tells you what time it is throughout the day. But once you pay more than fifty bucks for a watch, you are buying jewelry. You are buying a personal decoration that tells other people in a subtle way that you are successful.

Perhaps the deepest of *all* needs is the need to feel important, valued, worthwhile, both to ourselves and in the eyes of other people. When you can structure your product offering to enhance the status, respect, and prestige of another person, you can touch on this deep human need and can often trigger buying desire.

Emotions distort evaluations.

When you can appeal to a basic emotion, you can trigger buying desire so intense that the concern about price becomes secondary, or even irrelevant.

For example, it has been demonstrated that some men who are anxious to please a particular woman for romantic reasons lose almost all ability to make rational spending decisions. This is why they purchase expensive jewelry, perfume, gifts, bouquets of flowers, and even costlier items when they are under the influence of the strong emotions of love or desire.

5. Health and Fitness

Everyone wants to live a long time and enjoy great health. Economists predict that health products such as vitamin/mineral supplements and physical fitness equipment will be the next trillion-dollar industry. We all want to be healthier and to be thin and fit. We also want to have high levels of energy. And we want these same health benefits for our families. Consequently, we are attracted to products or services that will enable us to be thinner, more energetic, and in top form. If your product or service can enhance the physical quality of life of your prospect in a cost-effective way, people who are overtired, overweight, or have aches and pains will be extremely interested in talking to you.

6. Praise and Recognition

An important need shared by one and all is to be recognized for our accomplishments. As Abraham Lincoln said, "Everybody likes a compliment." One of the definitions of self-esteem is "the degree to which one feels praiseworthy." As a result, whenever someone receives praise and recognition for an accomplishment, large or small, that individual feels better and happier about him- or herself.

When you can position your product or service such that a person feels that he or she will achieve greater recognition or status by using it, you can create buying desire. Since the need for praise taps into that deepest emotional need of all, self-esteem, convincing your prospect that he will get additional recognition by using your product or service weakens his price resistance considerably.

> **Convincing your prospect that he will get additional recognition by using your product or service weakens his price resistance considerably.**

7. Power, Influence, and Popularity

There are many needs which you can demonstrate that your product or service will satisfy. People want power and influence and will buy products or services that will give them more of these things. People want to be popular and to be liked by other people. When your product or service offers to make a person more influential and popular, it arouses buying desire.

8. Leading the Field

Another of our deepest needs/desires is to be considered up-to-date. We want to be seen as current, modern. We want to be leaders and trend-setters in our work and social group.

Many people will buy your product or service simply because it is the *newest* product on the market. They want to be ahead of the pack. They want to be the first ones buying it and the first ones *with* it. In buyer segmentation, these are called "early adaptors." They represent 5 to 10 percent of the market. They will buy the product or service for no other reason than that it is new and different.

When you tell an interested prospect, "You will be the first person in your industry with this product," or "You will be the first person in your neighborhood who has one of these," you create immediate buying desire among early adaptors.

9. Love and Companionship

Today there are millions of subscribers to Internet dating services that match people with similar profiles. This is because people crave companionship and good relationships. An enormous number of people join clubs and associations to meet other people, especially those of the opposite sex. One of the primary motivators of social activities is the desire for love and companionship. When you can present your product or service as making the prospect more attractive and desirable as a companion, immediate buying desire is achievable.

10. Personal Growth

One of the greatest of needs associated with the twenty-first century is for additional knowledge and skill. People want to feel competent. They want to learn new skills and be on top of their jobs. They want to get ahead more rapidly. They want to excel and move ahead of their competitors, both within their companies and in other areas of their lives.

Many products appeal to the desire for greater self-understanding and self-actualization. That's because the needs for self-expression and personal fulfillment are profound. People want to feel that they are becoming *all that they are capable of becoming.* When you promote your product or service as something that can help people reach even greater heights of personal success and self-realization, you again generate a desire to purchase.

11. Personal Transformation

Perhaps the most abstract need, and the need for which people will pay the most, is the desire for *personal transformation.* If a prospect feels that your product or service will take him to a new, higher level in his life or work and make him a different person in some way, there can be no limit to the amount he will spend.

Not long ago I was talking to the vice president of a Midwestern manufacturing company. He is an avid golfer. He tries to play golf at least twice a week, and on vacation he plays five or six days a week, sometimes two rounds per day. He told me, "I would pay fifty thousand dollars *cash* for any golf pro who could show me how to permanently reduce my score by two strokes." This form of personal transformation, acquiring a new skill in an area important to him, was worth fifty thousand bucks!

Sometimes people will pay vast amounts of money for plastic surgery, to improve their appearance, or to vacation at health spas where they will lose weight and become physically fitter.

A personal transformation is purely emotional. Becoming more and better than you have ever been before is a common desire and an intense motivator of buying action. Whenever you can market your product or service as being capable of bringing about a permanent transformation of some kind, in work or personal life, you can usually make the sale.

Buying Decisions Are Emotional

All buying decisions are emotional. In fact, everything you do is 100 percent emotional. The rule is that *people decide emotionally and then justify logically.* You use logic to *justify* and *rationalize* your decision once you have made it. When you say that you are going to do something because it is the "logical" thing to do, all you are saying is that you have more emotion invested in that course of action than in another.

People decide emotionally and then justify logically.

Humans have a wide variety of emotions. But it has been discovered that the *strongest* emotion operating at any particular moment will determine how an individual decides and acts at that time. For example, a person may have a desire for the improvement that your product or service offers. But his fear of loss or of making a mistake can be more intense than his desire for gain. If this is the case, he will refrain from buying. The stronger emotion will always win out over the weaker emotion.

Increase Buying Desire

The only way you can overcome the negative emotion of fear of loss that will *block* a sale is by increasing the positive emotion of desire for gain that will *trigger* that sale. Everything you do or say that *increases* the intensity of buying desire moves you closer to the sale. Simultaneously, everything you do that *lowers* the fear of making a mistake, or loss, moves you toward the sale as well.

Reducing Fear of Loss

Marketing guru Jay Abraham has helped companies sell hundreds of millions of dollars' worth of products by convincing them to offer unconditional guarantees of satisfaction on everything they sell. He is famous for recommending that you give a "better than money-back guarantee." In this type of offer, the customer is promised that not only will he get his money back if he is not satisfied, but he will also receive, or be able to keep, certain special bonuses and gifts that have considerable perceived value.

In one of our businesses, we offer a complete one-year personal and professional development program on entrepreneurship and financial success. The course runs over fifty-two weeks. We guarantee that participants will be delighted with the results, or they will get their money back. In addition, they will be allowed to keep more than three thousand dollars' worth of books, tapes, and video training materials that accompany the course. This is a very powerful offer.

Wanting to Think It Over

When a prospect says that he wants to "think about it" for a while before deciding, he is really saying one of two things about what you have offered him: First, he could be saying that he has no real desire to own and enjoy what you are selling. For some reason, you have not "connected" with him at such a level that he is convinced he will be better off with your product or service than he would be with the money that it would cost.

The second reason that a person may hesitate and put off a buying decision is because he is not sufficiently persuaded that he will actually get what you are promising. He is saying that you have not given him enough emotional reasons for him to make a buying decision. His fear of loss or of error is still greater than the potential benefits from your offering.

Focus on Value

In the process of *value selling*, you put all your emphasis on repeating and explaining the values and benefits that the prospect will receive if he buys what you are selling. Instead of reducing the price or offering a special deal of some kind, you focus your efforts on building value. It is only when the customer feels that the value he receives is greatly in excess of the cost that he will have to pay that a buying decision takes place. Always focus on greater value rather than lower price.

Selling to Small Businesses

Many people sell to small and medium-sized businesses. They deal with the entrepreneur who actually started and built his or her business. If these salespeople are not careful, they can easily slip into talking about the features and benefits of their products and services without taking the time to realize exactly what type of customer they are talking to.

Entrepreneurs are successful because they focus most of their energies on sales and on satisfying customers. They have very little patience for detail. They consider bookwork, accounting and finance as necessary evils, things that they have to do in the process of selling and delivering their products, therefore . . . talk about sales and profits.

If a salesperson visits with a business owner and tries to sell her computers and software that will improve her accounting department, her eyes glaze over. She loses interest immediately. Because she does not associate accounting with profitability, she is the wrong person for you to be talking to.

Entrepreneurs are interested in sales and cash flow. They are concerned with communicating with customers and delivering their products and services satisfactorily. They focus on the performance and reliability of what they sell. And they are attracted to revenues, profits, and growth. They are not interested in the internal details of their operations. To sell the very most of your products or services, you must focus your time, attention, and energy on finding out exactly what will cause this customer to buy.

The more time you focus on clearly identifying the specific needs that you can satisfy for a customer, the easier it is for you to structure your presentation and make a sale.

Selling to Retail Businesses

Businesspeople who buy products for resale are only concerned about one thing: *net profits*. If you are selling to businesses who are buying your products or services to sell in the course of *their* business operations, they are still only concerned with one thing: net profits. They are not concerned with what the product *is*; they are only concerned with what the product *does* and how it affects their bottom line. The most important benefit that a product or service can offer a retail business customer is an increase in net profits.

> **The most important benefit that a product or service can offer a retail business customer is an increase in net profits.**

Selling to Larger Businesses

Businesses only buy products that help them improve performance and productivity, cut costs and expenses, or boost cash flow and profits. You must be clear about the most advantageous results that your product or service can achieve for your business prospect in one or more of these areas.

What you sell may help the company to cut costs in some area. It may increase or improve productivity. It might enhance the performance of either equipment or people. Perhaps your product helps the customer get greater sales results or increases buyer satisfaction. If you can convince a business prospect that what you are selling can *make or save time or money* in excess of what you are charging for your product, you can make a sale. This is your key job in selling to businesses.

Emphasize the Ultimate Benefit

Once upon a time, a woman in one of my seminars, who was selling office automation systems, said to me, "I just can't seem to get appointments. I call them up and tell them that we do office automation consulting, and they always tell us that they are 'not interested.'"

She told me that because of her company's experience, they can usually save their clients a good deal of money if they have a chance to examine their facilities and make recommendations. I asked her exactly how she went about approaching likely prospects.

She said, "I telephone and I say, 'Hello, I'm Betty Dean, from Office Automation Services and we'd like an opportunity to come in and show you how some of our products can increase your efficiency and the smoothness of your administration.' But they always say things like 'No, thank you. I'm too busy; we don't have the time right now; we can't afford it; we don't have it in the budget;' and so on."

Reword Your Approach

This sales professional was making the mistake of trying to sell on the phone, rather than just getting an appointment to sell. I suggested that she try prospecting a little differently: "The next time you make an appointment, call up and ask to speak to the person in charge of administration. When you get through to him or her, say these words: 'Hello, my name is Betty Dean, and I'm with ABC Company. We've developed a process that can save you 20 to 30 percent of your office administration costs. It would take me about ten minutes to show you how it works, and you could decide for yourself if it is the sort of thing you are looking for.'"

She told me later that this simple change in her approach enabled her to get all the appointments that she needed. Her sales doubled and tripled. She was soon making more money than she had ever earned before.

Talk About What They Want

The reason for this result, which thousands of salespeople enjoy once they understand this principle, is simple. People are not interested in office automation products, computers, servers, wireless communications, cell phones, or anything else. Businesspeople are interested in making or saving money or time. They are interested in getting better results and increasing profit.

There are only two ways that a business can increase its profits. It can increase its sales and revenues, holding costs constant, or it can decrease its costs, holding revenues constant. Whatever you are selling, you must describe it in terms of how it either increases revenues or cuts costs, or both.

If you are talking to someone who is in charge of administration, he is interested in *cutting costs.* If you are talking to someone in marketing or sales, she is interested in *increasing sales* and the resulting income. If you speak to the person who owns the company, he wants to improve the *bottom line.* You must always talk about your product or service in terms of what the customer wants, not in terms of what you are selling.

How Does He Get Paid?

Here is a key to selling products or services to people in business: ask questions about what the person does and what *results* he is responsible for. What are the key performance indicators of his job? What does she get *paid* for? What results is he expected to achieve for the company? How is she appraised or evaluated by her superiors? These are key questions to ask and find out the answers for.

As we said before, people always seek improvement in their conditions. They will only take action on an offer if they feel that they will be better off as a result. In business organizations, people will only approve the purchase of a product or service if they feel that it will improve their *personal* positions in the organization.

For example, let us say that you are promoting a sales training system and are talking to the sales manager who makes the decisions in this area. The entire focus of your presentation should be on improved sales performance rather than on improved profitability. The sales manager is not rewarded on the basis of profitability but on the results of the salespeople. Focus on the benefits that this specific prospect will personally enjoy, rather than general benefits that have no effect on this prospect's results or rewards.

Business Versus Personal Benefit

Sales experts often differentiate between a "business win" and a "personal win." A business win is what the company gets as a result of using your product or service. A personal win is how the individual will benefit personally when your product or service is installed and working successfully. People in business will not buy until they see that there will be measurable benefits in both areas.

Take the time to identify how the prospect will be better off personally in higher income, greater convenience, or even additional prestige and respect from other people in his company. These can be the key factors that trigger the buying decision.

Uncovering Basic Needs

The key to conducting a basic needs analysis is to *question skillfully and listen carefully*. The very best salespeople dominate the listening and let the customer dominate the talking. The more you ask questions and listen patiently and attentively to the answers, the more the customer will open up and talk to you.

People think about themselves most of the time. All day long, no matter what is going on, people are thinking about their own problems and concerns. What is most important to each person is on the *top of his mind.*

When you ask questions and listen carefully, you trigger these thoughts and concerns. They then come up in the conversation.

The Freudian Slip

In psychoanalysis, this is called a *Freudian slip*. Psychologists have found that if you allow a person to talk about himself freely, eventually he will *slip*. He will blurt out what he is really thinking about at the moment. The job of the psychologist is to create the kind of environment where the patient feels comfortable expressing himself openly and honestly.

In a way, you are a traveling *sales psychologist*. Your goal is also to create a comfortable environment with your personality. You ask good questions and then listen closely to the answers. You lean forward, nod, smile, and make no effort to interrupt.

Use Open-Ended Questions

The best questions to ask to open up a conversation and get more information from a prospect are called *open-ended questions*. These are questions that begin with a pronoun or adverb, words such as *what, where, when, how, who, why,* and *which*. These questions cannot be answered with a simple yes or no. They require a more expanded answer, which gives you a greater opportunity to understand the true needs of the prospect that can be satisfied by your product or service.

There is a rule that "telling is not selling." Only questioning is selling. It takes no creativity to talk about your product or service. It takes a good deal of thought, however, to phrase your information in the form of a series of questions from the general to the particular.

Today, people do not want to be *sold*. They may want to buy, but they don't want to feel that they are being sold. The moment a prospect feels that he is being pushed to make a buying decision, he shuts down and loses interest.

The Person Who Asks Questions Has Control

As a rule, *the person who asks questions has control.* The individual who is answering the questions is controlled by the person who is asking them. Whenever you ask a question and listen attentively to the answer, you are controlling the directional flow of the sales conversation, which is as it should be. Whenever you are talking in response to a question from the prospect, the prospect has taken control of the conversation.

If a prospect asks you a question, rather than answering automatically (which most people do), pause, take a breath, and say, "That is a good question. May I ask you something *first?*"

In other words, you acknowledge the question. But you then ask a question of your own and take back control of the conversation. When you do this a couple of times, it will become so natural and automatic that the prospect will never even know what happened. And you will be back in control.

Position Yourself Properly

The very best salespeople today see themselves more as consultants and advisors to their customers than as salespeople. As a consultant, your job is to help the customer solve his problems with what you are selling. The very best sales consultants focus all of their energies on identifying the most pressing problem that the customer has that their products or services can solve. He then concentrates all of his efforts on convincing the prospect that he will definitely get the solution that he most wants.

Position yourself as a *friend* rather than as a salesperson, as an *advisor* rather than as someone who just wants to make a sale. See yourself more as a *helper* than anything else. Take the time to fully understand the prospect's needs, and then help the prospect to understand how and why your product or service will satisfy these needs better than anything else.

Learn and Teach

Position yourself as a *teacher*. When you ask questions, you learn the customer's needs. When you talk, you teach the customer how he can most benefit from what you are selling. When you approach every sales situation as a *friend*, an *advisor*, and a *teacher*, you will dramatically lower the stress involved in competitive selling. You will radically reduce the likelihood of failure or rejection. Both you and the prospect will feel more comfortable and relaxed.

> **When you approach every sales situation as a friend, an advisor, and a teacher, you will dramatically lower the stress involved in competitive selling.**

Pause and Listen

The sale takes place with the words, but the buying takes place in the silence. Many salespeople speak too loudly and too fast because they are nervous. They are uncomfortable with silence. They feel that they have to fill every single moment with some wise comment or observation on their product or service. But this is not the case.

When you are asking questions and advising the prospect regarding your product or service, be sure to allow moments of silence in the conversation. Allow the customer to reflect on and digest what you are saying. Don't rush. Be calm and relaxed. Allow the sales process to unfold at its own speed, without pressure or urgency. This creates the very best mental state for the customer to make a buying decision.

Present Your Idea As an Improvement

People are funny in some respects. They want things to get better, and yet to stay the same. This is especially true in selling and in buying a new product. Very few people want something completely new. Somehow, if it is brand-new and untried or untested in the market, it is too risky. It might not work. You might lose your money. This is why most customers are defined as "late adaptors." They wait until the product has proven itself before they start to buy it.

The way to deal with this natural resistance when you are selling a new product is to describe it more as an "improvement" than as something new or different. Explain new features as advancements in the technology, as forward steps, as developments that your company has added to make it even better and more useful for your customer than before.

Tell the Truth

Customers want the simple truth about a product or service. They want honest information about how it can help them improve their lives and businesses. At the same time, they resist and resent any kind of high pressure. The more you relax and focus on the needs of the customer and helping him to satisfy those needs, the more relaxed both of you will be. The more you concentrate on explaining the simple truth about what your product can do for the customer, the easier it will be for the customer to buy.

Customers are seeking honest advice to help them do their jobs more efficiently or live their lives better. The more you focus on how you can help your customer, the easier it is for you to sell and for the customer to buy.

Quality Is Not Enough

Many salespeople get stuck on the subject of *quality*. Their main argument for buying is that they are selling a quality product. But quality is never the *primary* reason for buying anything. Quality is a logical argument. People buy things emotionally, but quality is always based on logic.

What is more important than quality is *utility*. When a person says, "My product is the highest-quality machine in the business," it doesn't matter. The only thing that the prospect is interested in is, will it do the job for me? Will it do what I need done? Is it adequate for my purposes?

You can say that a Rolls Royce or a Mercedes is a high-quality automobile, but if all you need is a car to go back and forth to work, you don't need to buy one of them. Quality is not an argument.

Quality and Price Comparisons

The only time you can use quality as an argument is when you are comparing your product at a *higher* price to another product at a *lower* price. You have to show the prospect that there are definite reasons why he should opt for higher quality rather than lower price. You have to prove that the customer will be much better off with your product, because it is of higher quality, than he might be with another product of lower quality, even if it is cheaper.

If you are selling a snowmobile to an Alaskan, quality performance is a more important argument than price. If he drives the snowmobile out on the polar ice cap and the machine breaks down, he is going to freeze to death before he gets back. In this case, the cost of higher quality is more than justified by the benefits.

If you are selling a vehicle to someone who is going to drive it across the Sahara, it is very important that it be a high-quality vehicle. If it breaks down in the Sahara, where there are no people and no water, the traveler will die before he gets help.

Explain Why Your Quality Is Important

If additional quality is not necessary to get the job done for the customer, then it is not an important benefit. In explaining quality features in your product or service, you must always explain how they *directly* benefit the customer. The customer must see the direct relationship between paying more for higher quality and getting more back as a result.

All customers ask the same question in their minds: *So what?*

Whatever you say to a prospect about your product or service, imagine that he is looking at you and saying, "So what?" What the customer really wants to know is, what's in it *for me*? What is the benefit *to me* of the feature that you are explaining? Why is this particular quality important *to me*? Make sure everything you say to a prospect about your product has a definite benefit in it for the customer, and make sure that the customer clearly understands this benefit.

> **Whatever you say to a prospect about your product or service, imagine that he is looking at you and saying, "So what?"**

Suitability Comes First

The product you sell must always be the *most suitable* for what the customer needs at the time, before quality enters into the equation. An example of suitability before quality is the popularity of Japanese automobiles. Everyone knows that they are well made and they last for several years. Because they sell at reasonable prices, they tend to be ideal and appropriate for a large number of drivers. They also happen to give good fuel economy. And *in addition* to this suitability factor, they are of good quality.

But the quality always comes *after* the appropriateness and the utility have been demonstrated. This is why it is so important to ask questions and identify the needs of the customer in advance, before you begin explaining why your product or service is the ideal one for him at this time.

Everything Counts!

In selling, one of the foremost principles of all is this: *everything counts!* Everything you do helps or hurts. It adds up or takes away. It moves you toward the successful conclusion of the sale, or it moves you away from it. Nothing is neutral.

There is a "halo effect" in selling, and in all human relationships. Prospects assume that if one part of your presentation or work is of high quality, the rest of your product or service is probably of high quality. One good impression often enables you to create a halo of quality and professionalism. And everything counts.

Your Appearance Counts—A Lot

In this respect, your personal appearance and grooming extend to the quality of your product itself. Most of the contact that your company will have with the customer will be you personally. For this reason, the way you appear and behave is a critical factor in the buying decision. It satisfies the prospect's need for assurance.

A whopping 95 percent of the first impression that you make on a customer is determined by your *clothes*. This is because, in most cases, your clothes cover 95 percent of your body. When you are well dressed, properly groomed, shoes polished and looking professional, the prospect unconsciously assumes that you are working for an excellent company and you sell an exceptional product or service. Further, when you are punctual, polite, and fully prepared, you make a positive impression that spreads like a halo to everything you do and to the product or service you sell.

On the other hand, if the salesperson is late, unprepared, and poorly organized, the customer immediately assumes that "what you see is what you get." He or she takes for granted that the company is second-rate and that the product or service being offered is of poor quality.

The Best Companies

The very best companies have the best-trained and best-looking salespeople. Companies like IBM and Hewlett Packard interview prospective salespeople several times to be sure, in advance, that these are the right people to represent them in a competitive marketplace. They take prospective salespeople out to dinner to see how they use their utensils and how they handle themselves in a social situation. They meet their families to measure the positive or negative dynamics between and among the spouses. They interview these prospective employees both individually and in groups. They know that an enormous portion of the buying decision is going to be determined by the person who is actually selling the product.

Identify the Basic and Secondary Needs

Be able to identify the basic and secondary needs that your product can satisfy, and then demonstrate this to the customer. You do this by asking questions skillfully and listening carefully to the answers. Sooner or later, the prospect will become interested by asking questions about what the product does and how it works. This becomes your selling opportunity.

For example, in selling computers and software to businesses, amateur salespeople usually spend a good deal of time talking about all the different functions that their equipment will perform.

But the customer does not care. He wants to know if the product will *pay for itself,* and *how long* it will take before it pays for itself. The customer wants to know *how certain* he can be that the product will pay for itself. He needs to know if this is an intelligent business decision or not.

Put Him in the Spotlight

Instead of thinking about yourself, focus all of your attention on the customer. Since you can only think about one thing at a time, the more you focus on the customer rather than yourself, the more relaxed and confident you will become—and the more positive and animated *he* will become. Whenever you start to feel tense in a sales situation, immediately ask the customer a question about himself or his business, and listen to the answer.

Imagine that you are in a darkened room with the customer. There is a single spotlight on a swivel above the customer's desk. This spotlight is voice activated. Whoever is speaking causes the spotlight to swivel around and focus exclusively on him. Who is supposed to be in the spotlight, you or the customer?

Since the customer is the most important person, the spotlight should be *on the customer* most of the time. Whenever the customer is talking and replying to your questions, the spotlight is on him. Whenever you are talking about him and his needs, problems, or objectives and requirements, the spotlight stays on him. The instant you start talking about yourself, your product, your service, your company, or your life story, the spotlight swivels around and focuses on you. The customer is left sitting in the dark.

The more the spotlight is on him, the greater the possibility that you will make a sale. Keep the spotlight on you and your company, and the likelihood that he will buy becomes less and less.

Customers Buy Benefits and Solutions

People don't buy products; they buy *benefits*. They buy solutions to their problems. They buy ways to satisfy their needs.

So again, focus *all* of your attention on the customer. Ask questions such as:

- "What are you doing now in this area?"

- "How is that working for you?"

- "What are your plans for the future in this area?"

- "If you could wave a magic wand and have the perfect situation in this area, how would it be different from what you are currently doing?"

- "What would you have to be convinced of to go ahead with our product, or any product?"

The person who asks questions has control.

Reasons for Buying, or Not Buying

In every sale, there is a *key benefit* that the prospect is seeking. This is the one thing that the prospect must be convinced of before he can buy. Your job is to uncover this key benefit and then to convince the customer that he will enjoy this benefit if he buys your product or service.

At the same time, there is a *key objection* to every sale, the major reason that the customer will hesitate or decide not to buy. It is absolutely essential that you uncover this key objection and find a way to answer it to the customer's satisfaction.

Focus on the 20 Percent

We spoke about the 80/20 rule a bit earlier. In terms of buying your product or service, the 80/20 rule applies as well. Fully 80 percent of the buying decision will be concentrated on 20 percent of the benefits that you offer to the prospect. Sometimes the 90/10 rule is in effect; 90 percent of the sales decision can be based on 10 percent of the features and benefits of your product. Your job is to find out what they are.

If you talk too much about features and benefits that are in the bottom 80 percent of concern to the prospect, you will actually hurt your chances of making a sale. Even if your product is the best in the world in the bottom 80 percent of reasons why the prospect should buy, they will not convince him to go ahead.

But if you can focus all of your attention on the top 10 or 20 percent of benefits that your prospect will enjoy, and convince him overwhelmingly that he will get these benefits from your product or service better and faster than from any other choice, the sale becomes much easier.

The "Hot-Button" Close

This brings us to one of the most powerful of all closing techniques. It is called the "hot-button" close, and it is used over and over by the highest-paid salespeople. It is quite simple. As the result of asking questions and listening carefully to the answers, you finally ascertain the "hot button," the leading benefit that this customer seeks in your product or service. You then concentrate all your energy on convincing him overwhelmingly that he will get this key benefit.

The success of the hot-button close depends on your ability to discover the prospect's most important reason for buying. You then repeat it over and over again.

Concentrate on selling that one main point. Do everything to convince a potential buyer that he will get that one benefit that is decisive for buying action. Bring the whole decision to hang on that one question. Press the hot button over and over.

How do you uncover the hot button? Simply ask, especially when the prospect is hesitating or holding back, "Mr. Prospect, if ever you were to buy this product, at any time in the future, what would cause you to do it at that time?" Then remain completely silent.

When you make it a theoretical question, the prospect will often say, "Well, if ever I was to buy this product, I would have to be convinced of [the hot button!]." Like a Freudian slip, it will often fall out of the prospect's mouth. You are then charged with convincing him that he will get that benefit immediately if he goes ahead with your offer.

Fast, Cheap Market Research

Here is a powerful exercise that can *double* your sales in a very short time. Make a list of your last ten customers. Phone each of them and say these words: "Mr. Customer, I just wanted to call you and tell you how much I appreciate your buying this product from us. How is everything going? Is there any way that we can help you?"

The customer may or may not ask you a question or have a problem with the product or service. If he does, though, promise to take care of it immediately after you get off the phone.

Then ask, "Mr. Customer, may I ask you a question? You could have purchased this product or service from another company, but you bought it from us. Could you tell me exactly why you decided to buy from us rather than from someone else?"

This is a powerful market research question. Remain perfectly silent. Let the customer think about it for a few seconds before he replies. *Don't interrupt.*

The Great Discovery

Here is the remarkable discovery that you will make. If you call ten previous customers, probably 80 percent of them will give you the same reason that they bought from you. Very often, you were completely unaware that this was the real reason for the purchase decision.

Whatever the answer, write it down. From that day forward, whenever you meet with a new prospect, be sure to tell him, "Most of our best customers say that the reason they decided to buy from us was [the hot button]. Is this important to you?"

The Flowering Cherry Tree

There is a story about a real estate agent who takes a couple to show them a house. The house is not in particularly great shape, but as they pull up in front of the house, the woman looks past the house, and in the back-yard, there is a beautiful, flowering cherry tree.

She immediately says, "Oh, Harry, look at that beautiful flowering cherry tree! There was a flowering cherry tree in my backyard when I was a little girl. I've always wanted to live in a house with a flowering cherry tree."

They all get out of the car and go in to look at the house. But the salesperson has taken note of what the woman said.

Harry looks at the house critically. The first thing he says is, "It looks like we're going to have to recarpet this house."

The salesman says, "Yes, that's true. But from here, just look; you can see out through the dining room, and you are looking right at that beautiful, flowering cherry tree."

The woman immediately looks out the back window at the flowering cherry tree and smiles. The salesman knows that the woman is the primary decision maker when it comes to buying a house. So he focuses on her.

They go into the kitchen and Harry says, "This kitchen's a bit small, and the plumbing looks old."

The salesman says, "Yes, that's true. But when you look through this window while you're preparing dinner, you can see that beautiful flowering cherry tree in the backyard."

Next they go upstairs to see the rest of the house. Harry says, "These bedrooms are too small, and besides, the wallpaper is old-fashioned, and the rooms all have to be repainted."

The salesperson says, "Yes, but notice that from the master bedroom, you have that beautiful view of the flowering cherry tree."

By the end of the walk through the house, the woman is so excited about the flowering cherry tree that she can't see anything else. The buying decision is made. They buy the house because the salesman has identified the hot button: the flowering cherry tree.

> **In every product or service that you sell, there is a "flowering cherry tree."**

In every product or service that you sell, there is a "flowering cherry tree." If this is a real prospect for what you are selling, there is something in your product or service that the prospect really wants to enjoy. It is a benefit that the prospect really wants to have. Find out what it is by questioning and listening, and then assure the customer that he will definitely get that benefit if he buys from you.

ACTION EXERCISES

1. Make a list of the needs that customers have that can be met by your product; organize this list in order of importance to the customer. Build your prospecting and selling around these needs.

2. Conduct regular market research among your satisfied customers; find out what benefit your product offered that caused them to buy from you rather than someone else.

3. Determine the most important benefit your business customers are seeking, and then develop a way to explain that benefit in every sales conversation.

4. Identify the most significant gains or losses that your prospects could experience from using or not using what you are selling; emphasize them repeatedly.

5. Dress for success; buy and read a book on proper business dress, and then follow it so that you look like a complete professional when you visit a customer.

6. Develop a series of open-ended questions that you can use to control the sales conversation and uncover the true needs of the prospect; keep the light on him by asking and listening.

7. Position yourself as a friend, an advisor, and a teacher in every customer contact; focus on helping and teaching rather than selling.

In helping others, we shall help ourselves, for whatever good we give out completes the circle and comes back to us.

—FLORA EDWARDS

4

CREATIVE SELLING

A man to carry on a successful business
must have imagination.
He must see things in a vision,
a dream of the whole thing.
—CHARLES SCHWAB

Creativity is a natural characteristic of all top salespeople. Fortunately, your level of creativity is largely determined by your self-concept, by how you think and feel about yourself when it comes to creative activity. This means that you can increase your creativity with practice until it becomes an automatic and easy response to any goal you set for yourself.

Creativity is something that you demonstrate and use all the time. When you are trying to avoid a traffic jam on your way to an appointment by taking alternate roads, side streets, and alleys, you are engaging in highly creative acts.

When you are arranging a party or designing a sales presentation, you are acting creatively. If you are attempting to convince somebody of the goodness and value of your product, you are behaving creatively.

Even getting dressed in the morning, when you match your clothing—ties, shirts, blouses, dresses, slacks, shoes—together to make an overall impression, you are engaging in an act of creativity.

Your Beliefs Become Your Reality

The sad fact is that most people do not think they are particularly creative. They associate creativity with writing great pieces of literature or painting great works of art. However, creativity can best be defined simply as "improvement." When you improve anything by doing things differently, you are using your creativity, sometimes at a high level.

Because of the central role of your self-concept, the more you *believe* yourself to be creative, the more you will generate creative ideas. In selling, you are essentially creating business where no business existed before. By the process of prospecting, building rapport, identifying needs, presenting solutions, answering objections, closing the sale, and getting resales and referrals, you are engaging in extraordinary complex creative acts that are the wellsprings of our free enterprise society.

Three Ways to Stimulate Creativity

Creativity is stimulated by three key factors: (1) clear goals, (2) pressing problems, and (3) focused questions. You must use all three as often as possible.

The more intensely you desire to achieve a clear, specific goal, the more creative you will be in finding ways to accomplish it.

The more determined you are to solve a pressing problem, the more resourceful you will be in coming up with different solutions.

The more focused and specific the questions that you ask yourself, or that others ask you, the more innovative you will be in developing answers. You should use all three of these continually to keep your mind functioning at its highest level.

Practice Thinking Creatively

In selling there are several areas where you can increase your creativity with regular exercise and practice. The more creative you become in these areas, the more money you will make.

The first area where creativity is important is in *prospecting*. Your success in prospecting largely determines your income. And your ability to find more and better prospects is only limited by your imagination.

The second area where creativity is essential is in *uncovering buying motives*. You must be creative in questioning to find out exactly what the customer needs and what will cause this customer to buy.

This is a real test of your intelligence and brainpower. Prospects have automatic buying resistance to any sales approach. They don't want to tell you why they might buy your product. They know from experience that if you find out what they really want, you will probably be able to convince them that they will get it, and they will be too weak to resist your offering.

Discover New Product Uses

Your creativity is essential in discovering new product uses and applications. You have to use your brainpower to discover new ways to use your products and to create sales where no sales exist. Bringing together all the ingredients of a business transaction, including you, your company, the customer, the product or service, the price and terms, the delivery and installation, and everything else, is an extraordinarily complex act and requires creativity at a high level.

Your ability to use your creativity to overcome buyer resistance and answer objections is essential to your success. Finally, your ability to close the sale and get the customer to take action is critical in determining how much you sell and how much you earn.

Know What You're Talking About

Creative selling begins with a thorough knowledge of your product or service. The better you know and understand what you are selling, the more creative you will become in selling it. The more knowledgeable you are about why and how your product is superior to that of the competition, the better you will be in explaining it to customers and in overcoming their buying resistance.

Read, study, and memorize your product information. Find out what your competitors are selling, what they emphasize, and how much they charge. Become an expert in your market.

Become Excellent at Prospecting

The fastest way to increase your income is simple. It is the key to success in selling. "Spend more time with better prospects." This six-word formula is the recipe for high income in every market.

> "Spend more time with better prospects." This six-word formula is the recipe for high income in every market.

Creative prospecting is essential to your success. It begins with thorough planning and analysis, and starts with three questions: (1) What are the five to ten *most attractive features* of your product? (2) What *specific needs* of your prospective customer does your product satisfy? and (3) What does your company offer that other companies do not offer; its *area of excellence?*

1. What Are the Five to Ten Most Attractive Features of Your Product?

Do you know your product's most attractive features? List them in order of importance. Then go on to determine the following:

- Why should somebody buy your product *at all?*

- Why should somebody buy your product from your *company?*

- Why should someone buy your product from *you?*

You must be able to answer these questions clearly in your own mind before you get face-to-face with a customer.

2. What Specific Needs of Your Prospective Customer Does Your Product Satisfy?

What benefits does it offer? In other words, what is in it for the customer to purchase your product rather than someone else's product, or no one's product?

Write the most attractive features of your product down one side of a piece of paper. Then write the benefits that your customer will enjoy from each of these features next to them on the other side of the paper. Remember, customers do not buy features; they only buy benefits. They do not buy products or services; they buy solutions to their problems. They are not concerned with what goes into your product; they are only concerned about what comes out for them.

3. What Does Your Company Offer That Other Companies Do Not Offer?

What is your "unique selling proposition?" What is your company's or product's *area of excellence?* In what ways is your company, product, or service superior to anything else available in your market?

The greater clarity you have with regard to these answers, the more creative you will be in finding better prospects and making more sales to those prospects.

Four Keys to Strategic Selling

There are four keys to strategic selling that you must master if you want to join the top 10 percent of money earners in your field. These are *specialization, differentiation, segmentation,* and *concentration.*

1. Specialize!

With specialization, you determine exactly what it is that your product is designed to do for your customer. You may specialize in a particular result or benefit. You can specialize in a particular customer or market. You can specialize in a particular geographic area. You can specialize in satisfying a particular need better than anyone else. But you must be a *specialist* rather than a *generalist*.

Many salespeople have built their entire careers by specializing in a particular industry, a specific type of customer, or a distinct geographic area. How could this apply to you?

2. Set Yourself Apart—Differentiate!

In differentiation, you determine what it is that makes your product *superior* to your competitor's. What special benefits does your product offer to your customers that are not available anywhere else? In what areas are your products better than 90 percent of similar goods or services on the market?

In many cases, if the product you are selling is available elsewhere, such as with real estate or life insurance, the special differentiator that you bring to the sales situation is your own unique *personality*. There is only one person like you in the whole world. Most sales are made on the basis of the *feeling* that the customer has about the salesperson, more than any other factor.

3. Sort Out Your Market—by Segmentation

The third part of strategic selling is *segmentation*. Once you have determined your area of specialization, and what it is that differentiates your product from your competitors', your next goal is to determine exactly which customers can most benefit from what you do better than anyone else. Who are they?

Where can you find more of this ideal type of person or organization for your product? Think of running an ad for "perfect customers." How would you describe them?

4. Focus and Concentrate

The fourth part of strategic selling is concentration. This is perhaps the most critical skill that you can develop for success in any area, especially selling. It is your ability to set clear priorities and then to concentrate single-mindedly on only those prospects who represent the very best potential as customers.

In some cases, one prospect may be worth one hundred times the value of another prospect. The basic rule in selling is to always *fish for whales, not minnows.* Remember, if you catch a thousand minnows, all you have is a bucketful of minnows. But if you catch one whale, it can sink your entire ship.

After a sales seminar in Tampa not long ago, a salesperson wrote to me and told me that she had begun applying these techniques immediately. Within one week, she closed a sale that represented 58 percent of her quota for the entire year. She was absolutely astonished at what a difference it made when she concentrated all of her energies on her largest potential customer.

What customers or markets could be capable of buying enormous quantities of what you sell? Where are they, and how can you approach them?

Conduct Intensive Market Analysis

You can use your creativity to identify your biggest and best sales opportunities. This requires the regular and repeated use of focused questions like these:

Who exactly is your customer?

Make a list of all the qualities and characteristics that your ideal customer would have. What would be his/her age, education, occupation, income level, experiences, attitude, or need? The greater clarity you have in identifying your ideal customer, the easier it will be for you to find more of these customers to talk to.

Who buys your product or service right now?

Apply the 80/20 rule. Who are the 20 percent of your customers who represent 80 percent of your business? What do they have in common? How could you find more customers *just like* the very best customers you serve today?

Who will be your future customers?

Markets are continually changing, and you must change as well. Project ahead five years. Based on current trends, who are likely to be your best customers at that time?

What are the trends in your business and in your market?

What changes are taking place that may force you to change the way you sell or the people to whom you sell? In what direction is your market moving? How are your customers changing?

What new markets might there be for your product or service?

Who else could benefit from your areas of specialization and differentiation that you have not yet reached?

Why does your customer buy?

What advantages or benefits does he perceive in purchasing your product or service? Of everything that you offer to a customer, what parts of your product or service does your customer most appreciate and compliment? What are the "hot buttons" that cause your customers to buy? You must know the answers to these questions.

Who or what is your competitor?

Who are your major and minor competitors? What benefits do your prospective customers see in buying from your competitors? How could you offset these perceived benefits? How could you position yourself in such a way that people would buy from you rather than from your competitors? This is often the key to breaking open the entire market. When companies position themselves properly against their competitors, their sales often increase by hundreds of percents.

Apple Versus Microsoft

Apple Computer was the first company to crack the market for the small personal or business computer. They came out of the gate with a user-friendly personal computer and immediately took the lead in the market, selling hundreds of thousands of Apple Ones and Apple Twos.

Microsoft entered the market after Apple, determined to catch up and surpass Apple's sales volume. But instead of developing computers, Microsoft focused on software, on the operating systems, and encouraged other software developers to develop programs compatible with theirs.

The strategies of the two companies were completely different. Apple was determined to keep all its operating codes and hardware proprietary so that it could charge higher prices and make higher profits. At its peak, Apple was earning 49 percent net profit on sales, an incredible amount.

A Different Strategy

Microsoft, under Bill Gates and Steve Ballmer, decided to offset the competitive advantage of Apple's user-friendly software by opening up its codes to software developers worldwide. Simultaneously, with each new advance in technology, Microsoft lowered the price of its MS-DOS operating system. Rather than focusing on high profits per individual sale, Microsoft focused on volume sales with a lower profit per sale but a far greater number of sales.

By the time the dust had settled, Microsoft controlled 90 percent of the global PC market. After becoming a runaway success story, Apple was surpassed in the market, and never caught up. By 2004, Apple's market share was down to 3 percent, even though its products are judged by many people to be technologically superior to those of Microsoft. What or who is your competitor, and how are you going to position your products against them?

Ignorance Can Be the Problem

In some cases, your major competitor is not another company. It is ignorance. Customers simply do not know your product is available. It may be new. It may not be well-known. It may not be well advertised. Sometimes, the greatest obstacle you have to overcome is unawareness of what your product can do for a customer.

In strategic selling, you are always competing against someone or something. Whatever you are selling, there is an alternative available in your market. What you have to find out is what your prospective customers are considering and then position yourself in such a way that your customers conclude that your offering is superior to anything else available.

Selling in some respects is similar to warfare. Decisions in warfare are always made in consideration of what the enemy is doing or likely to do. Many of your most crucial decisions in selling will be determined by what your competitors are doing, or what they are likely to do.

What is your competitive advantage?

This is your area of differentiation that we discussed earlier. In what way do you have an advantage over your competitors? How and why are you superior? As Jack Welch of General Electric once said, "If you don't have competitive advantage, don't compete!"

Your competitive advantage is invariably the most important reason that a customer would choose your product over that of your competitor. Fully understanding the nature of your competitive advantage is the key to developing an effective and creative sales presentation.

You should be so clear about the competitive advantage of your product or service that someone could wake you up at three in the morning, shake you, and ask, "Why is your product better than anybody else's?" and you could answer this question out of a sound sleep.

Your Area of Superiority

Customers buy a particular product or service because they feel that it is superior in some way to anything else available. Sometimes it is lower price. Sometimes it is a particular feature or benefit. Sometimes it is because they like the salesperson better than the representative of another company. Sometimes the competitive advantage is that you are the first person who has explained to them how much they could improve their lives or work with your product.

Whatever it is, the customer always chooses what he considers to be the very best available under the circumstances. Demonstrate to the customer that *your* product or service fits that description.

Same Old, Same Old

Not long ago, a young man came up to me at one of my seminars. He needed advice. He worked for one of ten companies that sold electrical supplies to contractors in the local market. But all of the suppliers bought their products from the same manufacturers and sold them at very much the same prices to the same customers. On top of this, the market for electrical products was depressed at that time.

He asked me, "Under these circumstances, how can I develop a unique selling feature or a competitive advantage?" I explained to him that it was not really possible. Based on what he had told me, he was selling something that anyone could buy somewhere else at the same price and quality, and on the same terms. His products had no unique selling features. In a depressed market, there was less business for everyone, including himself. There was very little future in his industry at that time.

Make Your Product Special in Some Way

One of the most creative things you can do is offer a product or service that is *special* in some way. It offers benefits that customers are willing to pay for that are not available anywhere else. If what you are offering is a me-too product, the only way you can sell more is by working longer and harder, by seeing more prospective customers, and by trusting in the law of averages. But there is no long-term future unless your product is unique and different in some way from any other product available.

Put Your Best Foot Forward

In creative selling, you always lead with the *most important* benefit that your product can offer your customer in comparison with your competitors. This becomes the key factor in your advertising, prospecting, and sales activities. When you meet a prospect who really wants the special benefits that only your product can offer, it is easy to make the sale.

Large companies spend an enormous amount of time and money to build a reputation for their *unique selling propositions*. When IBM was the biggest computer company in the world, it had an extraordinary reputation for *customer service*. The company invested more than one billion dollars per year in giving its customers fast, dependable service whenever an IBM product broke down. For major customers with large computer installations, IBM would often fly in several specialists from different parts of the world, all within twenty-four hours, to get a computer system up and running again. IBM's reputation for quality service made it an industry leader worldwide.

Interestingly, at no time did IBM ever have a *better, faster,* or *cheaper* product than its competitors. Other companies had superior products at lower prices with more features. IBM did not even attempt to lead the field with state-of-the-art equipment. They focused instead on their reputation for service and support. This competitive advantage enabled them to become the most successful company of its kind in the world.

It Takes Your Breath Away

Some years ago, the distributors of Smirnoff vodka attempted to introduce Smirnoff to the market in the United States. They had little success. At that time, vodka was considered not only a foreign drink, but a *Russian* foreign drink. The Cold War was on, and Americans were not particularly favorable to any Russian products, especially a new form of liquor.

The Smirnoff distributors spent an enormous amount of money attempting to position Smirnoff vodka as a superior choice to whiskey, scotch, gin, rum, and other liquors. But to no avail. Finally they identified the "unique selling feature" (USF) of Smirnoff: after drinking Smirnoff, no one could smell it on your breath.

They instantly created an advertising campaign around this USF with two lines: "Smirnoff! It takes your breath away" and "Smirnoff! It leaves you breathless."

In no time at all, Smirnoff became a $50 million product, and eventually a $500 million product. It broke the market open for vodka sales, which are now well in excess of a billion dollars a year. By identifying the competitive advantage of the beverage, that people could drink at lunch without folks back at the office knowing, they were able to create a great marketing success.

How could you describe or position your product in a similar way? What is your unique selling proposition?

Who are your noncustomers?

Who are the people who could use your product or service, but buy neither from you nor your competitors? These are people who are not even in the market at all. In reality, the noncustomers are the greatest untapped market for your products or services. If you can identify them and find a way to get through to them, you can often create sales where no sales exist and where there is little competition or price resistance.

A Huge Untapped Market

Often these people are the "late adaptors" in the market, those who wait until a new product or service has been tested and proven by the majority of buyers before they risk buying. When a company finds a way to tap into this huge late-adaptor market of noncustomers, it can often surpass all its competitors.

Three examples come quickly to mind: the fax machine, the personal computer, and the cell phone. In each case, only a few people were willing to take a risk on this new technology. In their earlier versions, they were often large, clumsy, and inefficient. The first cell phones often required a briefcase to carry them around.

But once these three innovations had been accepted by business-people and used in offices, the dam began to crack. Suddenly the non-customer entered the market by the millions. Today even children have computers, fax machines, and cell phones, which they are constantly upgrading with newer, better, faster, and cheaper versions. What were once early-adaptor markets have become multibillion-dollar worldwide markets. How might you apply this to your product or service?

The Nonvoter

Here is another example. The biggest noncustomer in our society today is the person who does not vote. The nonvoter, if he could be moti-vated to vote for a particular party, could determine the outcome of virtually every election in the country. Forty percent of qualified voters never go to the polls. They are the largest single voting bloc in the country.

Why Don't They Buy?

The people who are not now buying your product, or anyone else's product, are the greatest source of new customers. If you can find out why they are not buying at all, you can often break into a brand-new market and sell more than you ever have before.

Keep asking, with regard to noncustomers, *why don't they buy?* What is it in their perception that holds them back from buying the product or service you sell? What objection would have to be overcome in their minds to get them to come into the market? What could you do to dispel the ignorance that they have of how much they could benefit? How can you remove the fear that is holding them back?

Very often, the simplest way to approach the noncustomer market is to identify a specific benefit that the noncustomer values and desires enough to want to own your product or service. Demonstrate to this prospect that he will definitely get the one benefit that would motivate him to buy, and then give an unconditional guarantee of satisfaction. By focusing on the key benefit and backing it up with strong guarantees, you can often break down the resistance that keeps your noncustomer from buying in the first place.

When do your customers buy?

When is the *best time* to sell to your customer? Is it a specific time in the business cycle, or a specific season during the year? Do customers buy when business is growing, or when business is declining? Some services are most appropriate when businesses are in difficulty. Other services are bought more readily when businesses are growing rapidly.

What season of the year do your customers buy the most? During what stage of the business cycle do they buy? Some products are most suitable for startup businesses. Others are better suited for growing businesses. And some work best for large companies that have stabilized or leveled off in the market.

What Triggers Buying Behavior?

Some people are *impulse* buyers. They buy immediately when the product comes out on the market. These are the same people who see the new movie the first night it is shown. They try the new restaurant as soon as it opens. They embrace the new fashion trends as soon as they appear in the stores. Approximately 5 to 10 percent of customers are like this. They will try it without really knowing whether it is good or not.

Many people only buy a product when it is clear from two to four years of history that the product is popular and well accepted. Many products do not begin to take off until they have been in the market for four or five years. It often takes this long for the mass market to gain sufficient confidence to begin buying the product in quantity. Think about personal computers.

> **Many people only buy a product when it is clear from two to four years of history that the product is popular and well accepted.**

There are many buyers who only come into the market when it is already mature. The product or service is approaching the end of its life cycle. It is being replaced by similar products that are faster, better, and cheaper. The profits to be made at this stage of the life cycle are fairly small.

Finally, there is the postmature buyer who only buys a product just before it is taken off the market.

What has to happen before your prospect will buy your product?

Often, a person will only buy a product, or try out a company or service, when she has received a recommendation from someone she trusts. Sometimes the prospect will only buy when she has spoken to another satisfied customer. Or the prospect has to get encouragement, reinforcement, or approval from another person before she feels comfortable enough to buy.

Here are two good questions to ask the hesitant prospect:

- "What would have to happen before you went ahead with this offer?"

- "What would you have to be convinced of to buy this product or service?"

The answers you get will often give you the key to the sale.

Use Testimonial Letters

One of the most powerful of all sales tools is the *testimonial letter.* When you say that your product is excellent and a good choice for the prospect, he immediately discounts your words because, after all, you are a salesperson. But when someone else who has purchased your product says that it is "good," the customer believes and accepts this assessment.

Some years ago, when I was building one of my businesses, I was continually struggling with prospects because I was relatively new in the market. Yet everyone I had worked with was happy with my services. So I took a solid week and visited each of my previous customers. I asked them if they would write me a nice letter telling me how much they liked my services and recommending them to other people.

Most of them agreed immediately. I followed up continuously until I had a three-ring binder full of testimonial letters in plastic page protectors. This changed my sales career.

My Winning Strategy

From then on, when I would meet with a prospect, one of the first things that I would say is, "Before we begin, let me show you some letters that I am particularly proud of, from some of my customers."

I would then hand my binder to the prospect and let him read through the letters. I found that people love to read testimonial letters. It is sort of like reading other people's mail. Later, I took a yellow high-lighter and highlighted the very best sentences in each of the letters so that they jumped out when the prospect read the pages.

It was amazing! Very often the prospect would look up from read-ing through the testimonial letters and say, "I'm sold. How soon can we get started?" My sales doubled, tripled, and quadrupled. In the first two months after I started using testimonial letters, I made more sales than I had in the previous year.

Many people will write you a testimonial letter if you ask for it. But sometimes they are so busy that they don't get around to it. In this case, offer to write the letter yourself and ask them to type it onto their own letterhead and sign it. It is amazing how many customers will do this if you ask.

Overcome Objections with Testimonials

If you get the same objection over and over, especially with regard to your high price or the fact that your company or product is new in the market, ask your satisfied customers to answer that objection in the text of their letter. Often you can write the letter for them with the answer to this objection.

For example, let us say that your product is more expensive than that of your competitors, and your customers continually bring this up. You would ask for or write a testimonial letter that says something like this:

Dear Brian,

I just wanted to write and tell you how happy we are with your product. When you first approached me, I was concerned about the high price. But since I have started using your product, the benefits and results I have achieved are far greater than the small difference in price I paid. Thank you for everything.

Sincerely,

A Happy Customer

That kind of a letter is worth its weight in gold. If you have half a dozen letters like that, you can double and triple your sales in a short time. Soon you will be selling to almost everyone you speak to.

The Best Advertisement

The most powerful of all forms of advertising in our society is "word of mouth." Eighty-five percent of all sales take place only after someone has said that the product or service is good. All other advertising is an attempt to get people to try the product or service so that the process of word-of-mouth advertising can begin.

> **Eighty-five percent of all sales take place only after someone has said that the product or service is good.**

In the movie industry, studios invest 80 percent or more of their advertising budget in the week of the movie's release. Their goal is to get as many people into the theaters as quickly as possible, either before moviegoers find that the movie is not very good or to stimulate word-of-mouth advertising that will fill the theaters later.

In 2004, both Mel Gibson's *The Passion of the Christ* and Michael Moore's *Fahrenheit 9/11* generated extraordinary word-of-mouth advertising, turning both movies into blockbusters that made fortunes for their producers.

When was the last time that you decided to go to a restaurant by looking in the Yellow Pages? Instead, someone *tells* you that he has been there personally and enjoyed the experience. Only then do you try it for yourself. Word of mouth is everything.

Be Sure to Ask

Your *satisfied customers* are your very best source of resales and referrals. If you take the time to ask them why they bought from you rather than from someone else, they will tell you. Once you know why your customers buy from you, you can then repeat these same reasons when you are meeting with a new prospect.

Call or visit a satisfied customer, someone you like and who likes you, and tell him that your company is conducting some market research. "We are talking to some of our most valued customers to find out how we can serve them better in the future. Would you answer a few questions for me?"

You then ask him questions such as the following:

- "Why did you decide to buy from us rather than from someone else?"
- "What specific value or benefit do you feel that you get from our product?"
- "How could we improve it in the future for you?"
- "What kind of customer do you feel could most benefit from our product?"
- "Is there anything special that our product [or service] does that you did not expect when you bought it?"

Never be afraid to ask.

If you ask your happy customers enough questions, and listen carefully enough to the answers, they will tell you everything you need to know to sell more of your products to more people, faster and more easily than ever before.

Practice "Mindstorming" Regularly

This is one of the most powerful ways to stimulate your creativity, alert you to new opportunities, and accelerate your success in your sales career. It is called the "20 Idea Method." When you begin using this method regularly and applying some of the ideas that you generate, you will increase twofold or more your income in the months ahead.

Here's how it works. Take a sheet of paper and write your biggest goal or your most pressing problem at the top of the page in the form of a *question*. For example, you could write, "How can I double my income in the next twelve months?"

You can even be more specific: "How can I increase my income from $50,000 to $100,000 per year over the next twelve months?"

Be Clear and Concrete

The more clear and specific the question, the easier it is for your mind to generate multiple answers to it. You use this mindstorming method primarily on questions for which you are seeking concrete, tangible answers.

For example, you would *not* write, "How can I be happier?" This question is so soft and vague that your mind cannot focus on it and generate specific, workable answers.

Once you have written out your question, you then discipline yourself to write out twenty answers to that question. You write them in the *personal, positive, present* tense. For example, instead of writing, "Make more calls," you would write, "I make five extra calls each day." The more specific your answers, the more ideas they will stimulate.

Write Twenty Answers—Minimum

Write a minimum of twenty answers to the question. You can write *more* than twenty answers if you like, but you must discipline yourself to keep writing until you have at least twenty answers. For some reason, the number 20 has a magical effect. Very often, the twentieth answer is the breakthrough idea that changes your career.

Once you have put down twenty answers, go back over your list of answers and select at least *one idea* that you will implement immediately. Do it now, this very minute. Don't delay. This is very important.

When you generate these answers and then take action on at least one of them, you keep the tap open for creative ideas all day long. As you move through your day, you will constantly have ideas and insights on how you can be more effective and get more done. Your mind will sparkle like lights on a Christmas tree. You will be more alert and aware. You will come up with solutions not only to your own problems, but to the problems of others, quickly and efficiently.

The Key to Wealth

Earl Nightingale, in writing about this idea, said that more people have become wealthy using this 20 Idea Method than any other method of creative thinking ever discovered. In my own experience, and in the experience of thousands of my students, this 20 Idea exercise is life transforming. Once you begin using it, you will start applying it to every problem or goal you ever have. You can use it to outline any project, large or small. You can use it to build a house, or to build a career. The results you get will be absolutely amazing.

Cumulative Results

If you were to pick a different problem or goal, or even the same problem or goal, and conduct this mindstorming exercise each morning, you would generate a minimum of twenty ideas per day. If you did this exercise five days a week, you would generate one hundred ideas per week. If you did this exercise five days per week for fifty weeks a year, you would generate *five thousand* ideas each year to help you be more successful.

If you then selected one idea each day and took action on it immediately, that would come to 250 ideas per year that you would be implementing in your life to help you move faster toward your personal and career goals.

The Big Question

If you were to implement 250 new ideas each year to be more successful, do you think this would have any impact on your life? Would your income increase? Do you think that one self-improvement idea per day might change your life so dramatically that it would be unrecognizable a year from now?

Marshall McLuhan once wrote that all you need is an idea that is 10 percent new to make a million dollars. It does not have to be the discovery of relativity or a major scientific breakthrough. It only has to be a small improvement on what is currently being done in some field and which gives you a competitive advantage. One small competitive advantage is enough to separate you from everyone else and put you on the fast track to success.

When you begin using this idea and developing twenty ideas each day, you will be astonished. You will become one of the most creative salespeople in your field. As a result, you will become one of the highest-paid people in your profession. Once you develop the regular habit of thinking creatively and applying your creative ideas, there will be no product that you cannot sell successfully and no goal that you cannot achieve.

ACTION EXERCISES

1. You are a genius; resolve today that you will use your inborn creativity to solve any problem, overcome any obstacle, and achieve any goal you can set for yourself.

2. Write your most important goal at the top of a page in the form of a question; write out twenty (20) answers to that question and then take action on at least one of them; do this every day.

3. Identify your areas of excellence and superiority in your product or service; what makes what you sell better than any competitive alternative?

4. Determine why your customers buy from you rather than from someone else. Which prospects can most benefit from what you do best?

5. Where are your very best concentrations of prospective customers? Decide how you are going to spend more time with them.

6. Differentiate your products or services in a meaningful way; find out why people buy your product, and then show them why your product is the best choice, all things considered.

7. Get written testimonial letters from your satisfied customers, highlight the best sentences, and then place them in plastic pages in a three-ring binder. Show these letters to every prospect.

Far and away, the best prize that life offers is the chance to work hard at work worth doing.

—THEODORE ROOSEVELT

5

GETTING MORE APPOINTMENTS

When a man has done his best, has given his all, and in the
process supplied the needs of his family and his society,
that man has made a habit of succeeding.
—MACK R. DOUGLAS

The most important rule for selling success is *spend more time with better prospects*. This rule contains just six words, but it summarizes your complete strategy to selling. The more time you spend with better prospects, by the Law of Probabilities, the more sales you will make and the more successful you will be.

Finding new people to talk to and then approaching them for the first time is one of the most challenging parts of selling. All advertising/promotion is designed to speed up this process, or to make it easier. Prospecting is also the part of selling that causes the most stress and frustration. More salespeople lose heart and give up what might have been a successful career because of their inability to master the skills of prospecting than for any other reason.

You Can Learn Any Skill

Fortunately, prospecting is a skill that you can learn. If anyone else is good at prospecting, that is proof that you can be good as well. You simply need to learn the strategies and techniques used by other top people and then adapt them to your own work until you feel comfortable with them. After that, your sales success is guaranteed.

By now you have done your creative thinking and analysis of your market. You have identified your major competitive advantages and your unique selling proposition. You know exactly the very best type of people to talk to, what to say, and why they should buy from you rather than from anyone else. You have loaded your gun and cocked it. Now you have to aim and fire.

This is the hard part. Now you have to contact, either by phone or face-to-face, a real, live prospect who has never seen you before. This is one of the most fearsome parts of selling—until you master it.

The Process of Prospecting

An ongoing analysis of your product and your market will give you a continuous stream of new prospects and prospect groups to call on. Your first contact with the prospect will begin the process, which will or will not conclude with the sale. Therefore, every word of your approach or introduction must be planned in advance to accomplish the following goals.

Break Preoccupation

Your approach must *break the preoccupation* of the prospect. Everyone you call on is busy and thinking about other things. They are completely involved in their own problems, work, family, health, business, or bills. Unless you can break through this preoccupation with your opening words, you never get a chance to make a sales presentation.

Some salespeople phone, introduce themselves, and begin talking about their product or service immediately. A better way is to introduce yourself and then ask, "I need about two minutes of your time. Is this a good time to talk?" Only when the prospect has confirmed that he has a couple of minutes to listen to you do you ask a question aimed at the result or benefit of what you are selling.

Sell the Appointment, Not the Product

Never talk about your product or price on the phone unless you can actually make and conclude the sale without seeing the prospect personally. This is an important rule.

Young salespeople, in their eagerness to get appointments, often blurt out details about their product in the first couple of sentences. If you do this, you will *kill the sale*. The prospect does not have enough information to seriously consider your offer. Instead, he will say, "I'm not interested," or "We are not in the market right now." You will end up talking into a dead telephone line.

Choose Your Words Carefully

When meeting the prospect for the first time, a salesperson will often start off talking about his product while the prospect is still on the phone, signing checks, shuffling papers, or doing something else.

The prospect's mind is a thousand miles away. He is not paying attention to you. You may be sitting there, but he is still preoccupied with everything that is going on in his life. Your job is to break this preoccupation before you begin speaking.

Your first words should be the equivalent of throwing a brick through a plate glass window. Develop an opening statement or question that gets his complete attention. This sentence should always be aimed at the result or benefit that the prospect will receive from your product or service, but does not mention the product or service itself.

Preoccupation Breaking Made Simple

Many years ago, there was a salesman who worked for Corning Glass. This was the year that the company introduced safety glass for the first time. This product contained a transparent plastic sheet between two pieces of glass, and as a result, it did not shatter the way most windshield glass did at that time.

This young salesman went out with his new product, and within one year he became the top-performing salesman of safety glass in North America. At the national sales conference, he received the first prize for sales performance and was invited to share his secret with the other salespeople present. They wanted to know, "How did you sell so much more safety glass than anyone else?"

Demonstrate the Benefit

He explained, "First of all, I got the factory to cut some safety glass into six-inch squares as samples. Then I got a ball-peen hammer, which I took with me on sales calls. When I walked in on the prospect, I would ask, 'Would you like to see a piece of glass that doesn't shatter?'

"Almost invariably, the prospect would say, 'That's not possible, I don't believe it.' I would then put the glass sample on his desk, take out the ball-peen hammer, and whack it. He would instinctively jump and throw up his hands to protect his eyes. When he looked down and saw that the glass had not shattered, he would be amazed.

"After that, it was simple. I would just ask, 'How much would you like?' take out my order pad, and begin writing."

Teach It to Everyone

Corning Glass was so impressed with this technique that the following year they bought ball-peen hammers for all their salespeople, provided them with samples of safety glass, and sent them out nationwide. The method really worked; they sold glass by the carload.

At the end of the year, at the next national sales convention, the young salesman, for some reason, was still head and shoulders above every other salesperson in the country.

Once again, they invited him up on the stage to receive his award as the top salesperson in the country. And again they asked him, "What is it that you did *this* year to outsell everybody else?"

Get the Customer into the Act

"Well," he said. "I knew that you were all going to use my method, so I had to come up with a new technique. Now when I go in to see the customer, I've got a ball-peen hammer in one hand and the sample of safety glass in the other. I ask him, 'Would you like to see a piece of glass that doesn't shatter?'

"He usually says, 'I don't believe it.'

"Then, I put the piece of glass on his desk and I give *him* the hammer and have *him* hit it. When he tries and fails to smash the glass himself, he is totally convinced. Then I write up the order."

Well Begun Is Half-Done

A good opening, with a strong question aimed at the result or benefit of your product, can get you almost to the close of the sale. A strong opening breaks the prospect's preoccupation, makes him fully alert, and gets you his complete attention. He is immediately willing to listen to you.

Marketing guru Dan Kennedy has a powerful technique for testing your opening sentence when you visit a prospect for the first time. He says that your opening words should trigger the response "Really? How do you do that?"

For example, "We can provide you with glass that doesn't shatter."

"Really? How do you do that?" Your statement should immediately grab his undivided attention.

Your Time Is Limited

You only have about thirty seconds at the beginning of your meeting to get the prospect's complete attention. In the first thirty seconds, the prospect decides whether or not he is going to listen to you. If you wander or make general conversation, the prospect will grow impatient. Within thirty seconds, he will have turned off and tuned out. It is then hard to get him back.

Experts generally agree that the first fifteen to twenty-five words out of your mouth set the tone for the rest of the conversation. You should select these words carefully and rehearse them regularly. They should not be left to chance.

> **The first fifteen to twenty-five words out of your mouth set the tone for the rest of the conversation.**

Many salespeople meet with a prospect for the first time and say to themselves, *I can hardly wait to hear what I have to say; I wonder what's going to fall out of my mouth next!* This is not for you.

Plan It Word for Word

Your opening question or statement should be planned word-for-word, rehearsed in front of a mirror over and over, and memorized. You then must go out and say it to a real live prospect. See what kind of response you get. If your prospect does not respond with interest and complete attention, it is back to the drawing board. You have to rework your opening question or statement until it gets the kind of reaction you want:

"Really, what is it?"

Cold-Calling for Appointments

I learned about the importance of this from my own experience. When I was selling sales training, I would call people on the telephone and say something like, "I would like to talk to you about training your salespeople."

This automatically triggered responses such as

- "We can't afford it."

- "We don't have the time to train our salespeople."

- "We have our own sales training program."

- "Our people don't need training."

- "Sales are down right now, and we can't pay for it."

- "Business is bad."

- "We don't have any training money in our budget."

With some variation, these are the same things that prospects tell us all the time.

Rewrite and Reword Your Opening Words

When I found that I wasn't getting anywhere with my approach, I sat down and studied it. I spent several hours working and reworking my opening comments, trying to determine how I could cold-call on prospects in sales organizations more effectively.

I finally realized where I was going wrong and developed a strategy to compensate for it. The first thing I decided was that I had to be sure that I was speaking to the right person before I made any attempt to set up an appointment.

Who is the prospect for sales training in a business organization? It was obviously the person who was responsible for making decisions about sales training for the salespeople: the owner or sales manager.

My second question was, *what is the basic need or concern of my ideal prospect?*

This, too, was obvious. My ideal customer was *not* interested in sales training. He was interested in higher sales volume, in increasing sales results. I realized that I had to ask a question that focused on that specific need, the result or benefit that my ideal prospect was seeking.

Back to the Phone

I began prospecting by telephone once more. My first question was to the receptionist: "Who is the person in your organization that is responsible for sales and sales training?"

"That would be Mr. Brown, our sales manager."

"Could I speak to Mr. Brown, please?" And the receptionist would put me through.

When I got through, I would say, "Mr. Brown, my name is Brian Tracy. I'm with the Institute for Executive Development. I was wondering if you would be interested in a proven method that could increase your sales by 20 to 30 percent over the next twelve months?"

What kind of response do you think I got? Almost every prospect answered, "Of course. What is it?"

Repeat the Key Benefit

I would then repeat the key benefit, or "hot button." "Mr. Brown, we've developed a method to increase your sales by 20 percent, 30 percent, and even 50 percent over the next few months."

The prospect would often say, "Really? How do you do that?"

My response would be, "That is exactly why I am calling you. I just need ten minutes of your time to show you this system, and you can decide for yourself if it applies to your company and your salespeople."

From failure and frustration in telephone prospecting, I began getting appointments with four out of five, and even nine out of ten people that I called cold, out of the phone book. With this simple change in my approach, I did more business in the next two months than I had done in the previous year.

Your opening question should trigger the response "What is it?" or "Really? How do you do that?" If it does not generate such a response, then you need to rework the question. If it is not breaking the prospect's preoccupation and getting his complete attention, you must reword the question until it does.

Sales Resistance Is Normal

If the prospect says, "Well, I'm not really interested," it means one of two things: either your question is not strong enough, or the person that you are talking to is not a prospect for what you are selling in the first place. You are probably talking to the wrong person.

When you open with a strong statement or question, you separate yourself into an elite class of sales professionals. Instead of wasting the first couple of minutes talking about your product line and how long you have been in town, you go straight to the subject that is of most interest to the prospect.

Neutralizing Initial Sales Resistance

Whenever you phone a prospect for the first time, you are *interrupting* him from something he is doing that he considers to be *more important* than anything you have to say. Everyone is busy. For this reason, you should always expect initial sales resistance, even if you are offering the very best product at the very best price to the most qualified prospect in the world.

Here is a simple technique that you can use to neutralize sales resistance at the very beginning. When the prospect says something like "Thanks for calling, but I'm not interested," or "We're not really in the market right now," you shouldn't take it seriously. The prospect has no idea how good your product or service can be for him and his company. His reaction is a knee-jerk, automatic response to any sales offer. Roll with this resistance, like a boxer rolls with a punch, and come back with these words:

"That's all right. Most people in your industry felt the same way when I first called on them. But now they've become our best customers, and they recommend us to their friends."

When the prospect hears these words, he immediately stops what he is doing and starts paying attention. He will almost invariably say, "Oh really? What is it then?"

Customize Your Comeback

You can make these words even more powerful by being specific about the prospect's *occupation*. You can say, "That's OK. Most people in the financial services industry felt the same way when I first called on them. But now they've become our best clients, and they recommend us to their friends."

In Robert Cialdini's book, *Influence*, he explains the impact of "social proof" in building credibility and arousing desire. Social proof comes from other people, like the customers who have already bought the product or service. Whenever we hear of someone else like us, in our business or with our same interests or beliefs, who has bought a product, we are immediately interested in knowing what it is. If lots of people like us have bought a particular product, we almost automatically conclude that it is a good choice for us as well.

When the prospect says, "Oh, really? What is it, then?" you say, "That's exactly what I would like to talk to you about, and I just need about ten minutes of your time. You can decide for yourself if it's right for you."

Frequently, busy prospects will say, "Well, can you tell me a little bit about it on the phone?"

Don't Sell on the Phone

You reply, "Mr. Prospect, I'd love to tell you about it on the phone, but I have something I have to *show* you. You need to see it personally."

This triggers the powerful emotion of *curiosity*. You should immediately offer two time periods to meet, "Would Tuesday morning be convenient for you? Or would sometime on Wednesday afternoon be better?" Remember, the purpose of your first call is not to sell or even to discuss your product or service. It is to get a ten-minute face-to-face appointment with the prospect. Do not talk about anything else but this appointment, and absolutely refuse to discuss your product or price on the phone.

Sidestep the Excuse

Sometimes the busy prospect will say, "Could you send me something in the mail?" If you send the prospect something in the mail, the chances are very high that he will lose it, forget about it, or decide not to see or talk to you at all. He will feel that he has enough information to make a decision and that he doesn't have to tie up his time with a salesperson. Sending things in the mail is usually a complete waste of time and money, unless you are selling from a distance.

When the prospect asks if you could mail something, respond by saying, "I would love to mail it to you, but you know how undependable the mail can be today. Why don't I drop it off to you personally on Tuesday afternoon when I'm in the area? Will you be available at that time?"

Don't Be Put Off

The prospect may now make a last-ditch effort to avoid committing: "All right, why don't you call me on Monday and we can set up a specific time to get together next week?" If you accept this "put-off," then when you call on Monday, the prospect will be in a "meeting" from which he will probably never emerge.

Instead say, "Mr. Prospect, I've got my calendar here in front of me. Do you have your schedule handy?"

The prospect will always agree that he has his schedule near at hand. You then say, "Let's set up a specific time right now. If something comes up and this time doesn't work for you, you can give me a call and we can reschedule. Would Tuesday afternoon at around three o'clock be convenient for you?"

When the prospect agrees to meet with you at a *specific* time, you have made your *first sale*, the sale that makes the *real* sale possible. You then confirm by *repeating* the time, day, and date of the meeting, plus you give the prospect your telephone number in case something comes up. Once this has been done, thank the prospect; repeat the time, date, and place of the meeting; and say, "Thank you; you are really going to like what I have to show you."

> When the prospect agrees to meet with you at a specific time, you have made your first sale, the sale that makes the real sale possible.

Face-to-Face with the Prospect

Your first selling task is to get the prospect to *listen* to you. Before the prospect will relax and listen to you, she wants to be sure of five things. She may not say it or ask for these five factors by name, but they are essential if you want to get a fair hearing.

First, she wants to be sure that you have something important to communicate. That is why you go straight to the result or benefit of what you sell in your first sentence. If what you are offering is relevant to her life or work, you will have her complete attention.

Second, she wants to be sure that you are talking to the right person. Since your product or service usually solves a problem of some kind, she wants to be sure that she is the one with the problem or need that you can solve or satisfy.

Fortunately, you have already qualified this prospect when you got through to her via the receptionist. You already know that you are talking to the right person.

But if you have any doubts at all, ask her, "Are you the person that I would talk to about increasing sales in your organization?"; "Are you the one with whom I should speak about cutting your costs of information processing?"; or "Are you the person to talk to with regard to [the specific need or problem] within your organization?"

Remember, you do not sell a product or a service. You sell a solution to a problem or the satisfaction of a genuine need. You must initially find the person who has the problem or the need. Only then can you begin talking about helping her get the benefits of what you are selling.

There is no point in doing a wonderful sales presentation to someone to whom your product is of no interest or who is not in a position to make a buying decision. Always be sure you are talking to the right person.

Third, at least initially, the prospect wants to be assured that your visit will be *short.* People are extremely busy today. They are often overwhelmed with problems and responsibilities. They become nervous and negative if they think that someone is going to take up a lot of their time. You must therefore assure them right away that you are only going to take up a couple of minutes to tell them about the benefit you have mentioned in your opening question.

Fourth, the prospect wants to be sure that she will be placed under *no obligation* if she meets with you. This is why you say, "I have something to show you, and you can judge for yourself." This takes the pressure off the prospect and often determines whether you get the appointment in the first place.

Fifth, the prospect wants to be sure that you will not use *high pressure.* The two most common fears of prospects, with regard to salespeople, are the *fear of being pressured* and the *fear of being taken advantage of.* By approaching the prospect with a positive, polite, and friendly attitude, you take these fears away. You cause her to relax and listen to you more closely.

You have to accomplish these five goals at the beginning of your conversation, and often on the phone with a new prospect, just to get the appointment. There is a method for doing this that I have taught to thousands of salespeople. When they have used this method, it has often revolutionized their results in getting appointments either by telephone or while cold-calling.

Begin with a Well-Structured Question

When you finally get face-to-face with a new prospect, introduce yourself, shake hands, sit down, and begin by asking a well-structured question. This is often an interesting or unusual question aimed at the benefit of what you are selling.

Questions are powerful, because each person is conditioned from childhood to answer questions when they are asked. If you ask a person what time it is, before he can think of anything else, he will look at his watch and tell you the time. People respond automatically to questions.

This is why we say in selling that "the person who asks questions has control." The person who is asking the questions controls the person who is answering. The very fastest way to take control over any conversation is to pause and ask a question. Until the other person has answered your question, he will be totally focused on what he is saying.

When you ask the prospect, "May I ask you a question?" he will almost always say yes. You will then be in complete control.

Continue Asking Questions; Good Questions Trigger Good Responses

When you ask the prospect, "Would you like to see a proven method to increase your sales by 20 to 30 percent per year?" the prospect cannot say anything else until he has answered the question. The questioner is in control.

In all my years of opening a call with a prospect using this question, I have only had one person who has said, "No, I'm not interested." And the reason he wasn't interested was that the receivers in his bankruptcy had just come in and closed the company down. He said on the phone, "It's too late for us; I wish you had called me six months ago."

But every other sales manager to whom I have asked that question has said, "Yes. What is it? When would you like to come in and talk?" Your question should trigger this response as well.

The second step in this method of getting face-to-face appointments is to be courteous and say, "I would just need about ten minutes of your time to show you what I've got, and you can judge for yourself."

The essential point to convey is "you be the judge." This assures the prospect that the meeting will be brief, he will be under no pressure, and you have something important and relevant to share with him.

Refer to Other Happy Customers

In most cases, even with the best opening question, prospects will be reluctant and resistant to making an appointment with you. To overcome this resistance, the most powerful technique is to refer to other satisfied customers who are already using your product.

If you are calling on a printing company and you have already sold one of your products to another printing company, tell them, "Another company in your industry, ABC Printing Services, is already using this product and is getting great results."

Because of the power of *social proof,* this often changes a negative or neutral prospect to positive and triggers a desire to see you and learn about what other people in that industry are already doing.

Build the Credibility of Your Product

When I was selling sales training, I would say, "Hundreds of companies are already using this process and are reaping great results. It is proven, practical, and completely guaranteed. And I just need ten minutes of your time to show it to you, and you can decide for yourself."

Anyone can give you ten minutes. They may not be able to give you half an hour before the month after next, but they can give you ten minutes right away if you have something that is of interest to them.

Be Professional at All Times

It is important that you don't make the mistake of offering the prospect a choice of two specific times, such as "Would 10:30 this morning or 11:20 tomorrow morning be best for you?"

This is an old, manipulative method of getting appointments that customers have heard so many times. If you use it, you hurt your credibility. Even if the prospect is interested in your offering, he may lose interest if he feels you are trying to manipulate him.

This is the time when you must be pleasant, positive, and persistent. Offer the prospect a choice of general times, like around ten on Wednesday or three in the afternoon on Thursday. If neither of these times will work for the prospect, ask, "When would be a convenient time for you?" *The person who asks questions has control.*

Confirm the Appointment

Once you have made an appointment, the job is not done. It is only beginning. Before you go off to a prearranged appointment, always call to reconfirm. This is a mark of top professionals.

Many people are afraid to call and confirm because they fear that the prospect will cancel the appointment. So they just show up at the scheduled time. Often however, the prospect has been called into a meeting or out of town. Sometimes he or she is sick or has had an emergency. A large number of prearranged appointments fall through for reasons over which you have no control.

There are two ways to confirm an appointment. The first is to call through to the prospect and tell him that you will be there at the scheduled time and are looking forward to seeing him. This gives the prospect an opportunity to reschedule if something has come up that conflicts with your meeting.

Another way to confirm an appointment is to simply call the receptionist and ask, "Is Mr. Brown there?"

When the receptionist says, "Yes," you then say, "Good, this is Brian Tracy. I am just calling to confirm my appointment with him at ten o'clock tomorrow morning. Please tell him that I will be there on schedule. Thank you very much."

If for any reason your appointment is canceled, move immediately to reschedule it at a specific time, using the techniques that I explained earlier in this chapter. I have often set up and confirmed appointments at a specific time, several weeks in advance. It is amazing how many of these prearranged appointments come off on schedule and how much business eventually comes from them.

Manage by Exception

The prospect will often say, "I am not sure that I will be in town on that day. Could you call me back in a few days or next week to set something up?"

When you hear this, you immediately respond with "Mr. Prospect, I know how busy you are. But let's manage by exception. We'll set a firm appointment now, and if anything comes up later, we can change it at that time."

Be polite, but be persistent. Once you have an opportunity to speak to an interested and qualified prospect, you must be insistent on nailing down a specific time to meet with that prospect.

Human beings are strongly affected by their expectations. If they expect to learn or to benefit from meeting with you, they will be looking forward to your appointment. If there is a need to reschedule, they will usually call you if you have set it up correctly at the beginning.

Your chances of making a sale once you get face-to-face with the prospect increase by ten or twenty times over a telephone discussion. Once the prospect has an opportunity to meet you, see you, look you in the eye, and realize that you are a knowledgeable, professional person, he is much, much more likely to take you seriously.

Improve Your Telephone Prospecting

There are two things you can do to improve the quality of your telephone prospecting. The first is to *stand up* when you speak to the prospect. When you stand up, you align all the energy centers of your body. The strength and tone of your voice will sound stronger and more confident. You will have more energy. You will sound more believable and authoritative.

The second thing you can do is *smile into the phone* when you speak. Surprisingly, a smile can be "felt" on the other end of the line. (People also know when you are not smiling, or even worse, when you are frowning.)

Many salespeople with whom I work actually set up mirrors on their desks and smile into them when they are talking on the phone to their prospects. When you combine standing up with smiling, you project greater energy and sincerity. It is often just the extra push that you need to get the appointment over the phone.

Keep the Initiative

Never expect people to call you back, no matter how honest or intelligent they sound. You as the salesperson must always maintain the initiative until you get the first face-to-face appointment. Don't let people put you off for any reason and then expect them to get back to you at a later time. Because they are so busy, they will never get around to it, even if they are interested in what you sell.

> **Never expect people to call you back, no matter how honest or intelligent they sound.**

Remember, *rejection is not personal.* Initial sales resistance is not personal either. When the prospect says that he is not interested or that he is already satisfied with his existing situation, it doesn't mean anything. It is a normal and natural response to your call. Don't take it personally.

Practice Mental Rehearsal

Here is one of the most important success secrets of all in the psychology of selling. It involves the way you prepare mentally immediately before going in to see the prospect, especially for the first time.

Stop for a few seconds and create a clear mental picture of yourself as completely relaxed, calm, positive, smiling, and in complete control of the interview. Then inhale deeply, filling up your lungs and putting pressure on your diaphragm. Hold this breath for a count of seven and exhale for a count of seven. While you are breathing deeply, continue to hold a picture of yourself as the very best salesperson you could possibly be.

Create a Clear Mental Picture

Then, just before you go in to see the prospect, create a picture in your mind of the prospect responding to you positively. See him or her smiling, nodding, agreeing, and enjoying your presence and your conversation.

You can increase the power of mental rehearsal prior to a sales meeting by remembering a previous successful sales call. Think about the best sales call that you have had recently. Think about how much you enjoyed talking to the prospect, how positive the prospect was, and especially, the presentation ending with a sale. Remember the feelings of happiness and satisfaction that you got from that transaction.

Then transfer the same feeling to the mental picture that you have created for yourself and the prospect you are about to see. This exercise will amaze you. It will smooth out your whole personality. By breathing deeply, relaxing, and visualizing, you will be fully prepared to perform at your best.

Talk to Yourself Positively

Don't forget to use the technique we covered earlier: the use of positive affirmations. Especially if you feel a little tense, repeat to yourself, strongly and emphatically, the words "I like myself! I like myself! I like myself!" Say, "I love my work! I love my work! I love my work!"

Help yourself warm up and prepare mentally by repeating, "I feel happy! I feel healthy! I feel terrific!" It is not possible for you to talk positively to yourself, using words like this, without immediately feeling happier and more confident. When you walk in to see the prospect, the prospect will feel the positive energy coming from you.

Always prepare for a sales meeting by breathing, visualizing, and affirming in advance. It will make all the difference in the world.

Set the Stage Immediately

When you meet with a prospect, shake hands firmly and say, "Thank you very much for your time; you are really going to enjoy what I have to show you."

When you build positive expectancy, you get him interested and make him curious. He begins saying to himself, *I wonder what it is.*

When you are smiling, confident, and positive, you project this to the prospect and create a high level of anticipation in what you have to say.

Expect to Be Welcome

Sometimes your prospect has had a bad morning. Ever since she arrived, she has been deluged with phone messages, e-mails, and complaints. The coffee was cold. Her employees are sick or unhappy, and her boss is mad. Then you come in. The prospect thinks, *Thank heavens, here's a nice, pleasant, intelligent, positive-looking person who's got something interesting to tell me.*

Many people feel this way. You could be the highlight of the entire morning or afternoon. When you are pleasant and smiling, they will be happy to see you.

Refuse to Talk Standing Up

When you arrive at your appointment, sometimes a busy prospect will come out to meet you in the reception area and ask you to tell him about your product. But you should refuse to make your presentation standing up. If you do, you run the risk of devaluing your product or service. No one buys a product or service standing up. Refuse to sell it that way.

> **No one buys a product or service standing up. Refuse to sell it that way.**

Remember the adage: *everything counts!* Unless you sell in a showroom, nobody considers a product or service of any value if you are willing to talk about it and try to sell it standing up. Instead, say, "What I have to show you is really important, and I need about ten minutes of your time."

If the prospect does not invite you to sit down to discuss your offering, say, "If you don't have the time right now, perhaps we could schedule ten minutes at a later date when it would be more convenient for you."

But refuse to discuss your product or service standing up. The basic rule is this: if the prospect cannot *buy* your product standing up, don't try to *sell* it standing up.

Respect Your Product

The same is true for the telephone. If your prospect cannot buy what you are selling over the phone, don't try to make an over-the-phone sale. If the prospect cannot buy and pay for it through the mail, don't try to sell it through the mail. If selling your product requires your being there physically, then insist on being there personally to make the sales presentation.

People don't make buying decisions standing up. They make buying decisions sitting down, where they are comfortable, in their offices or their homes. They make buying decisions after listening, considering, reflecting, and looking at your material. They only buy after they have evaluated, reviewed, and decided that the benefits you offer are worth more than the price you charge.

ACTION
EXERCISES

1. Determine exactly the number of prospects you must call each day and each week to achieve your sales and income goals.

2. Spend 80 percent of your time prospecting until you have so many people to see that you do not have time to call anyone else.

3. Write out your script for telephone prospecting, memorize it, and practice it continually until it sounds natural and relaxed.

4. Ignore initial sales resistance when you prospect; focus on the result or benefit of what you sell, and refer to other happy customers who already use it.

5. Keep the initiative; nail down the exact date and time of your first appointment with the prospect.

6. Refuse to talk about your product or service, or the price, on the phone; focus single-mindedly on getting a face-to-face meeting, nothing more.

7. Prepare thoroughly for every sales meeting; do your homework, on the Internet if possible, so you look and sound like an absolute professional when you meet the prospect for the first time.

Meticulous planning will enable everything a man does to appear spontaneous.

—MARK CAINE

6

THE POWER
OF SUGGESTION

*Whatever we plant in our subconscious mind and nourish
with repetition and emotion will one day become a reality.*
—EARL NIGHTINGALE

Human beings are greatly influenced by the suggestive elements in
their environments, especially the human elements. The suggestive
influence of a calm, confident, relaxed salesperson is very powerful. This
is why the most successful salespeople are usually those who are the most
tranquil and easygoing. They are usually well dressed, well groomed, and
professional looking in every respect.

Top salespeople have a calming, soothing effect on customers. They
have confidence in themselves and in their product or service. As a result,
we feel confident in listening to them. We feel convinced about the things
they say and about the product or service they offer.

The External Environment

Each person is strongly influenced by his physical environment as
well. Your environment has a tremendous impact on how you think, feel,
and behave. Small changes in your environment can bring about immediate changes in the way you react and respond to what is going on
around you.

For example, normal room temperature is about seventy degrees

Fahrenheit. But if you raise or lower this temperature by five degrees, it can dramatically change your level of comfort and the amount of attention you give to what is being said. If you are too hot or too cold, your discomfort will lead you to be irritable, demanding, and impatient.

The People Around You

In your suggestive environment, perhaps the most powerful influence of all is the people that you deal with. You are very strongly influenced by the way people respond to you and behave when you are around them.

Much of your reaction to other people is initially *subconscious.* Everyone has experienced meeting a person and instantly having a negative or positive reaction to him or her, even before a word has been exchanged. The reason for this instant assessment is that your previous experiences with many other people are stored in your subconscious mind as part of your permanent memory bank. When you meet a new person, your subconscious *connects the dots* and gives you an instant assessment of that person, based on your previous experiences.

You respond subconsciously to other people; customers respond subconsciously to *you.* Everything you do prior to the sales presentation, and everything about you when you meet the prospect, either increases or decreases the quality of the suggestive environment and determines whether or not you make a sale.

Your Internal Environment

There are several suggestive influences that you can control. The essentials are your *appearance,* your *voice,* and your *attitude.*

If you look good, your voice is clear and confident, and your attitude is calm and optimistic, the initial impact of your presence will make a positive impression on the prospect.

Fortunately, you can control your physical appearance in almost every respect. You can dress professionally, groom yourself attractively, and control your posture. Your goal at all times is to look on the outside as if you were one of the very best people in your field.

Practice Your Selling

You can assure that your voice is strong and clear by practicing your presentation aloud in front of a mirror. Professional actors spend many hours walking, talking, gesturing, and delivering their lines before a mirror, exactly as if they were attempting to project their voices to the back row of the audience. Then, when you are with a prospect, you simply turn down the volume while maintaining the same confidence and energy. This has an inordinate suggestive influence on the mind of the prospect.

Be Positive and Cheerful

You can control your attitude, making sure that it is upbeat and confident, by using the mental rehearsal techniques already mentioned. You can visualize yourself regularly as one of the top sales professionals in your field. Before you go in to see the prospect, you can talk to yourself positively, repeating, "I'm the best! I'm the best! I'm the best!" You can stand erect, with your back straight and your chin up. You can look the prospect in the eye and shake hands firmly. You can come across as a positive, prepared, professional salesperson in every respect.

Dress for Success

One of the turning points in my sales career came when a friend of mine took me aside and asked me if I had ever read anything about the proper clothes to wear when I met with a customer. I came from a family where no one ever wore a suit, and no one ever told me about the importance of dress in business. But I was a ready student.

My friend explained a few things about dressing for success in business. Later I bought a series of books on the subject and studied dress extensively. What I learned was that 95 percent of the first impression you make on a prospect will be determined by your clothing.

Prospects Are Visual

Prospects are intensely visual. The visual impact of your clothes strikes the prospect like a wave hitting a breakwater, and exerts a strong subconscious influence on that prospect. The way you look on the outside is considered to be an expression of the kind of person you are on the inside.

> **The visual impact of your clothes strikes the prospect like a wave hitting a breakwater, and exerts a strong subconscious influence on that prospect.**

When you are well dressed and groomed, the customer unconsciously assumes that you come from a good company and that your product or service is of good quality. When you look the part of a top salesperson at the first meeting, the prospect takes you more seriously and is more open to your sales message.

Who Makes the Most Money?

Over the years, in more than a thousand seminars with more than a million salespeople, I have noticed that the best-dressed salespeople are always the ones making the most money in their fields. Whenever a well-dressed salesperson talks to me, it is immediately evident from his confident attitude that he is making excellent money in his field.

On the other hand, I see countless salespeople who have no idea that they are sabotaging themselves and their sales each morning when they leave the house dressed poorly. The tragedy is that no one has ever taken them aside and explained to them how important appropriate business dress is to success. Worse, no one wants to criticize a salesperson by telling him or her that his or her dress is not appropriate. Everyone knows, but no one says anything.

Every salesperson should read at least two books on proper business attire and then follow their advice religiously. Remember, in dress, as well as in all other aspects of selling, everything counts! It is either helping you or hurting you. It either adds or detracts. Your dress either moves you toward the sale, or moves you away. Dress is one of the most powerful of all suggestive influences in selling.

The Friendship Factor

One of the most notable truths in sales, which I have already addressed briefly, is this: "a person will not buy from you until he is convinced that you are his friend and acting in his best interest."

Another point in Robert Cialdini's book, *Influence,* is the importance of "liking" in sales success. If a prospect likes you, the details will not get in the way of the sale. But if the prospect is neutral or negative toward you, the details will trip you up every step of the way and often make a sale impossible.

The first unspoken question a customer asks when he meets you for the first time is "Do you care about me?" If you do not answer yes in the first minute or two, the customer will quietly lose interest in doing business with you. He may sit politely through your visit and your presentation, but at the end, he will thank you for coming in and tell you that he will "think about it."

We like to deal with people toward whom we feel friendly. We set the stage for this relationship in the first few seconds of the first conversation, and with the first few words.

Hair Care

The focus of the sales conversation should be on the face of the salesperson. For this reason, grooming is of the essence. The rule is that nothing about your grooming, or your dress for that matter, should distract from the message that you are there to deliver.

You've heard the saying "birds of a feather flock together," or "like attracts like." The fact is that we like to deal with people, and buy from people who are similar to us in as many respects as possible. We feel more comfortable with people who dress the way we do, groom the way we do, have the same attitudes and opinions that we have, and so on. The more you harmonize your appearance so that it is in keeping with the way people look in the customer's environment, the less resistance the customer has to listening to you and doing business with you.

One of our greatest desires is to feel comfortable in a personal or business situation. Everything you do that increases the level of comfort of your prospect also increases the likelihood that you will make a sale to him or her.

Long Hair, Short Sales Record

Some years ago, a young salesman approached me at a seminar and asked me for advice on increasing his sales. I saw immediately from his long, shaggy hair what his problem was. When I asked him about his business, he told me that his primary customers were businesspeople in offices. He had a good product at a good price, but he wasn't making very many sales. The reason for this was immediately evident to me.

I told him that if he wanted to be more successful in selling to businesspeople, he would have to cut his hair. He flared up and said that his hair length should not make any difference. He liked to "express his personality" by wearing long, shaggy hair, over his collar. I explained to him that he could wear his hair as long as he wanted, but he was trading long hair for sales success.

Immediate Action, Immediate Results

Fortunately, he was a good student. He went out and got his hair cut, but only a little bit. Nonetheless, his sales increased almost immediately.

So he cut his hair even shorter. Again, his sales increased noticeably. He finally went all the way and got a conservative, businesslike haircut. His sales jumped.

He was able to move out of his parents' house, get a car, and begin creating a good life for himself. He was delighted.

But alas! He began to think that his success was solely because of his great product and exceptional personality. He reverted to his old ways and started growing his hair longer and longer. And as his hair grew longer, his sales slowed down once more.

When his hair was once more over his collar and he looked like a shaggy dog going from prospect to prospect, he ran out of money and had to move back home with his parents. The last time I saw him, he still had long hair. He wore old clothes and had holes in his shoes. He trudged from appointment to appointment with little hope, and even less success.

Presenting Your Product

Your product or service should always be clean, neat, and presented in its best possible light. People are strongly influenced by the suggestive impact of a product that is colorful and attractive. Prospects are negatively influenced by product materials that are dirty, dingy, peppered with coffee stains, or sloppy and disorderly. Always take the time to assure that your sales materials look excellent in every respect. Remember, people are highly visual. What they see has an inordinate impact on the opinions they form of you, your product or service, and your company.

Practice Your Presentation

Your sales presentation should be well organized, practiced, and complete with all details. As much as 80 percent of the value of your product or service, as far as your prospect is concerned, will be contained in the quality of your presentation. If your sales presentation is random and wandering, the prospect will consider your product or service to be less desirable or attractive.

If your presentation is crisp and well-ordered and moves step-by-step in a logical process, the customer will assume that your product, your service, and your company are equally ordered and efficient. A professional sales presentation can dramatically increase the perceived value of what you are selling and simultaneously lower price resistance.

Pleasant Surroundings

Your surroundings should always be clean, orderly, and emanating success and prosperity. When people come to your place of business, they should immediately get the feeling that this is a successful organization. Everything should be tidy and in its place.

In our Advanced Coaching Programs, we train successful entrepreneurs to make changes in the images that they present to their customers. The results our clients have achieved are often astounding.

Recently a couple with a small business complained that, though they were quite successful in getting prospects to come to their office for an initial sales interview, afterward the prospects went away and never came back. These two very talented people were constantly working on upgrading and improving their sales presentation and materials, but to no avail. Something they were doing, or failing to do, was costing them an enormous amount of business.

Upgrade Your Offices

It turned out that they had started their business working out of their home. When they decided to move from their home, they rented an inexpensive office and set it up with used furniture. Just as I had not known how to dress properly as a salesperson, they did not know how to lay out a business office. Because no one had given them any advice, their office looked cheap and secondhand.

When prospects came in, in response to their sales and marketing activities, their first impression was that this was a second-rate company. The office looked and felt low budget. No matter how positive and cheerful they were in dealing with their customers, prospects could not get over the negative suggestive impact that the appearance of the office was having on their subconscious minds. They left and never returned.

Take Immediate Action

Our coaching classes are held every ninety days. Once this couple understood the importance of the visual impact that their offices were making on their clients, they resolved to completely redecorate, get new furniture, put in new carpets, hang art on the wall, install a professional music system, and have fresh cut flowers in their reception area. They went back and implemented these ideas immediately.

When they returned to the coaching class after ninety days, they were bubbling with excitement. Their closing ratio had jumped from about 5 percent to about 50 percent. They had tripled their sales and profitability. They were absolutely amazed at the impact that their attractive and well-appointed offices had on their prospects. They received countless compliments from their new customers on how beautifully their offices were laid out. They had more than paid for the cost of redecoration within thirty days from additional sales and profits.

Work from a Clean Desk

One of the rules of office etiquette is "keep your desk clean!" When you have a neat desk and an orderly office, you look like a successful person. On the other hand, when your desk is cluttered with all sorts of things, you look confused, disorderly, and incompetent. People conclude that it would be unsafe to do business with you.

You should only have one thing on your desk at a time, the one task that you are working on at the moment. Everything else should be put away, in drawers, on the credenza behind you, or in files. You can even clear your desk by putting everything in a stack, and putting the stack on your floor behind the desk. But keep your desk clean.

Double Your Productivity

In my extensive work on time management and personal productivity over more than twenty years, I have found that people who work from a clean desk are two or three times as productive as those who work from a cluttered desk. When you work from a clean desk, you can focus and concentrate on one thing at a time.

> **People who work from a clean desk are two or three times as productive as those who work from a cluttered desk.**

When your desk is cluttered, you are constantly arranging and rearranging papers and work. Most of the time, you are unsure where everything is. You spend an enormous amount of time going back and forth, getting little done. Single focus is the key to high productivity, and a clean desk is the key to single focus.

Create an Impression of Value

When you look like a total professional, well dressed and well groomed, and your sales presentation is organized, efficient, and effective, the customer gets the unconscious feeling that you are selling a valuable product that is worth every penny you charge. As the customer's confidence in you and your company increases, his or her price resistance declines.

First-class companies, represented by first-class people, find it much easier to charge higher prices than their second-rate competitors.

The Way You See Is the Way You Will Be

To succeed, you must see yourself as a complete professional in every respect. Treat yourself, and your customers, as if you were one of the best-educated and most knowledgeable people in your business.

Think of the behavior of an accountant or management consultant. In each case, these professionals do not start off talking to you in a random fashion. They have a series of questions that they ask you, in order. They seek a specific quality and quantity of information that they request from you in a systematic way. And the more they focus on asking that series of questions about you and your situation, the more confident you feel in doing business with them.

You Are a World-Class Professional

Imagine yourself as a "doctor of selling." The more time you spend asking your "patient" logical, intelligent, well-organized questions, the more he feels that he is in the presence of a professional. His initial sales resistance and skepticism decline. His confidence in you increases. He relaxes and opens up. He realizes that you are there to help him solve a problem or achieve a goal. He begins to work with you rather than hold back from you.

Walk the Talk

Body language is also important in selling. According to Albert Mehrabian of UCLA, the message you convey in a sales conversation is 55 percent body language, 38 percent tone of voice, and only 7 percent in the words that you use. Because people are highly visual, they are most affected by the predominant message that you convey, and this is usually communicated by the way you hold and use your body.

When you walk, imagine that your head is dangling from a string, holding your entire body erect. You should breathe deeply with your shoulders back and your spine straight. Raise your chin and look straight ahead.

Walk and move with strength and confidence. Pick up the pace. Don't shuffle along. Move fast, as if you have places to go and people to see. Your overall physical impression should be one of a busy, active, confident, and effective sales professional.

Shake Hands Firmly and Fully

When you meet people, give a strong, full, firm handshake. This initial physical contact can often make or break the sale for you. When people feel your hand, they measure your character. When your handshake is strong and firm, they assume that you have good character and, by extension, represent a good product or service.

Some salespeople that I meet give weak, indifferent handshakes, as if offering a cold fish. Others, especially women, give a "half handshake," offering their fingers instead of a full handshake. This suggests that you are dealing with a "half person."

Not long ago, a gentleman came up to me at one of my seminars and asked me why he was having so much trouble in his sales work. He was quite proficient at getting appointments over the phone, but immediately after meeting the prospect in person for the first time, the sales conversation seemed to deteriorate.

Something You Can't Hide

As soon as he shook hands with me, I knew the problem. He was originally from India, from a culture where people did not shake hands when they met. As a result, when he held out his hand to a prospect, his grip was weak and sloppy. The prospect immediately lost interest in him and his product, and he could sense it.

No one had ever told him this. He had no idea how important a firm handshake was in initiating a business contact in our culture. He had thought that shaking hands was merely a formality that had no meaning. When he learned that a handshake was important, he began to practice giving firm, full-handed handshakes to everyone he met. He wrote to me later and said that his sales had jumped from the very first week that he began practicing this new technique.

The Proper Greeting

Someone once wrote a letter to "Ms. Manners," asking if the proper greeting upon meeting a new person was "Pleased to meet you," or "How do you do?"

Ms. Manners replied by saying that the correct greeting is "How do you do?" Humorously, she added that you do not say, "Pleased to meet you," because you don't yet know if you are.

When you meet a prospect for the first time, offer your hand, look the prospect directly in the eye, and say, "How do you do?" This initial contact is like the kickoff in a football game. If it is done properly, it can move you a long way down the field toward the goalposts of a successful sale.

Sit Erect, Facing Forward

When you sit in a sales situation, always face the prospect directly. Never lean against the back of the chair. This makes you look relaxed and uncaring about the purpose of your visit. Instead, sit with your back erect. Lean forward slightly. Stay alert, and be fully engaged, both physically and mentally, in the sales conversation. You should look like a runner at the mark, waiting for the starting gun.

Interestingly enough, we are greatly influenced by the body language of the people to whom we speak. When you are sitting up straight, leaning forward, and aware of your surroundings, you cause the prospect to be more interested and aware as well. He or she will pay closer attention to you and be more involved in your sales message. At an unconscious level, the prospect assumes that what you have to convey is important and valuable. That individual will therefore pay closer attention to you than if you were leaned back and relaxed during the sales conversation.

Get the Prospect to Open Up

If a prospect is sitting with his or her arms folded, this is usually not a good sign. Occasionally it is because the office is too cold, but in most cases it is a sign of disinterest. When a person's arms are folded, it usually means his mind is closed. Folded arms are an unconscious body-language way of blocking out incoming information. When he unfolds his arms, he opens his mind.

Get the prospect to unfold his arms. It is fortunately quite simple. To open the client up to your message, begin by asking questions. If he does not relax and unfold his arms, hand him something physically, like a brochure or price list to read. Ask him to calculate a number or give you a business card. Use your ingenuity to get those arms unfolded so that he is more open and receptive to you and your message.

Use Positive Body Language

Crossed legs can be sending the same message. When a customer's legs are crossed, it usually means that he is holding back information. If his legs are crossed at the ankle, it means that he is not telling you everything that you need to know.

In the process of "mirroring and matching," your prospect will tend to mimic your own body language. When you deliberately keep your arms unfolded and your hands open, with your feet flat on the floor, ankles uncrossed, your prospect will often engage in the same body language.

When you lean slightly forward, listen attentively to what the prospect is saying, nod, smile, and listen, the prospect will often engage in the same behaviors. He or she will soon begin speaking, asking questions, and listening more attentively as well.

Minimize Noise and Interruptions

People can only concentrate on one thing at a time. This is why it is so important to minimize the noise and distractions in the environment while talking to a prospect. Try to ensure that there are no interruptions. If you are in your prospect's place of business and there is a lot going on around you, ask if you can move to a location where you can speak for a few minutes without interruptions. Say, "Mr. Prospect, I only need about ten minutes of your time. Is there somewhere we could sit where we wouldn't be interrupted?"

You will be happily surprised at how many prospects will immediately agree to this.

Avoid Barriers to Communication

When you sit with the prospect, try to avoid barriers, like tables or desks. If the prospect is sitting behind a desk, ask him if you could sit together at a table where you can more easily show him the material that you have brought with you. I have never had a prospect refuse to get up and move if a salesperson asked him to do so in a polite and pleasant way.

When you sit next to a prospect, always have the individual sit on your left. In this way, when you turn the pages of your presentation material, it is easy for the prospect to see everything you are doing. When you ask the prospect to move, and he agrees, he begins the process of responding to your reasonable requests. This moves you closer to the point at which you can ask for the sale.

Selling in the Home

When you are selling in the home, there are certain special psychological dynamics to which you must pay attention. First of all, never make a sales presentation in the living room. People do not make important business or family decisions in the living room; they make them in the kitchen or at the dining room table. These are the places where they talk about business matters that affect them.

Even though you are invited to sit in the living room, say instead, "Why don't we sit at the kitchen table, where we will be more comfortable?" Then stand. The suggestive influence of a professional salesperson standing up, waiting to be led to the kitchen or dining room table, is very powerful, and almost irresistible.

Wait to Be Seated

When you get to the kitchen or dining room table, wait for them to show you where to sit. Each person has a favorite chair at the table where they sit each day. You must be sure that you do not seat yourself in that chair. When you sit at the table, make sure you can maintain eye contact with both people. When you ask questions and explain your product, continually alternate the person you are speaking to so that both people feel fully involved in the presentation.

Always Be Polite

Finally, with regard to etiquette, whether in a place of business or at home, never forget your manners. Always be courteous and considerate with prospects, their employees, their spouses, and with other people in the office.

When you go to your appointment at a place of business, always treat the receptionist with courtesy and respect. Treat everyone as if he or she is really important and valuable. Behave toward each person as if he or she is a million-dollar customer or has the potential to become one.

The Reward for Treating People Well

Perhaps the greatest benefit of all from treating people well is this: whenever you do anything to raise the self-esteem of another person, your self-esteem goes up to the same degree. When you are polite and respect-ful, you like and respect yourself more, while causing other people to like and respect themselves more at the same time. The more you practice these critical suggestive elements in selling, the more powerful, positive, and confident you become, and the higher your sales will be.

ACTION
EXERCISES

1. Everything counts! Take complete control of every factor that your prospect sees, hears, feels, and does; plan in advance.

2. Visualize yourself as a "doctor of selling," as a world-class professional, thoroughly knowledgeable, with an excellent product or service.

3. Dress for success; pattern your dress after the most successful and highest-paid people in your business. Look like the kind of person that a customer can confidently take advice from.

4. Be courteous with everyone you meet, from the receptionist through to the secretary and customer; always be positive and cheerful.

5. Practice mental rehearsal before every sales call; imagine yourself as calm, controlled, optimistic, and completely relaxed; the way you see yourself is the way you'll be.

6. Do everything possible to avoid noise or distractions of any kind when you are talking to a prospect; have him move if necessary so he can concentrate on you and your product.

7. Walk erect, chin up; shake hands firmly and confidently; carry yourself as if you are the best in your field.

By visualizing your goals, you can get your subconscious mind to work toward making those subconscious pictures come true.

—SUCCESS MAGAZINE

7

MAKING
THE SALE

Any fact is not as important as our attitude toward it,
for that determines our success or failure.
—NORMAN VINCENT PEALE

E verything you do in the sales process, from the first contact through to the close of the sale and the delivery of the product or service, has an effect. Nothing is neutral. Everything either helps or hurts. Nothing can be left to chance. It all counts.

The first words out of your mouth begin the process that leads to either a sale or a rejection. When you meet a prospect for the first time, his or her level of sales resistance is at its highest. In fact, all prospects have what is called "generalized sales resistance" at the beginning of any meeting with any salesperson under almost any circumstance. This is a normal, natural part of living in a commercial society. It is a form of self-defense.

Self-Defense Against Sales Messages

The average customer is exposed to perhaps three thousand commercial messages a day, from all sources. From the time he gets up in the morning, he is bombarded with sales messages on the radio, television, billboards, and store signs; in newspapers and magazines; and in telephone calls and mail solicitations. Everywhere he turns, there are advertisements shouting, "Buy this!"

To survive in a commercial society, a person must develop a high degree of sales resistance. First, he must filter out most of these messages, ignoring them, if for no other reason than to be able to function effectively. Second, he must be able to resist direct sales approaches from salespeople like you, or he will end up buying everything that is offered to him. As a professional, learn to expect this generalized sales resistance in your first meeting and to deal with it effectively.

The Approach Close

One of the most helpful ways to begin a sales conversation is with the "approach close." When used successfully, this close can get the prospect to agree to making a decision after you have made your presentation. Rather than his saying something like, "Well, let me think about it" or "I need to talk it over with someone," you can ask for a decision, one way or the other.

You reduce initial sales resistance by saying, "Mr. Prospect, thank you very much for your time. Please relax; I'm not here to sell you anything right now. That's not the purpose of my visit."

If you deliver this opening statement with a smile, the prospect will relax a little. He will still be suspicious, but not as much as before.

You then say, "All I want to do in the time we have together is show you some of the reasons why so many other people have bought this product and continue to buy it. All I ask is that you look at what I have to show you with an open mind, determine whether or not it applies to your situation, and then tell me at the end of our conversation whether or not this product makes sense to you. Is that fair?"

With this "approach close," you are offering an exchange. You are saying, "I won't try to sell you anything if, in exchange, you will listen with an open mind."

A Fair Exchange. Almost without fail, the prospect will agree to your offer. He has nothing to lose. In fact, he is now curious to know why so many other people have purchased your product and continue to purchase it. His mind is open, and he is prepared to listen to you.

There is a very strong *suggestive* element involved in this close. You are *suggesting* that the product is already popular and being used by a great number of people. All that is being asked of the prospect is that he agree or disagree that the same reasons that other people are using what you sell apply to him.

You then begin your sales process by asking questions to find out what he is already doing and how your product or service might apply to his situation. Like a "doctor of selling," you conduct a thorough examination to uncover needs that the prospect has that your product or service can satisfy.

Once you are clear about the prospect's situation and needs, you can present your product as the ideal solution to his needs at this time, all things considered. At the end of your presentation, you have the psychological advantage.

Ask for an Answer. If the prospect says, "Well, I have to think it over," you can respond by saying, "Well, Mr. Prospect, I appreciate that, but you promised you would tell me one way or the other if this applied to your situation or not."

You then say, "And after what you've told me, it seems that this is ideal for you at this time, unless there is something else that I don't understand."

This forces the prospect to give you a reason for hesitating or objecting. In either case, this allows you to answer the objection and to go on selling. But when a prospect ends with "I want to think it over," there is nothing you can do. You cannot continue selling unless you have an objection that you can answer. By using this approach close, you force the prospect to give you an objection, which you can probably handle.

You can use this approach close with virtually any product or service. When you suggest that large numbers of customers have already bought this, and continue to buy it, you build a high degree of positive expectancy right at the beginning. You trigger the prospect's curiosity. You get him to listen to you with an open mind and to give you any reasons that might cause him to hesitate at the end rather than putting you off with "Let me think it over."

The Demonstration Close

This is a powerful closing technique that you can use early in the sales conversation. It often sets up the conditions necessary for you to make a sale at the end of your presentation.

The demonstration close starts with a strong question aimed at the chief result or benefit that the customer would enjoy when he buys your product, and simultaneously qualifies the prospect.

When I was selling mutual funds, this method was very effective. I would open with the question, "Mr. Prospect, if I could show you the best investment available on the market today, are you in a position to invest five thousand dollars right now?"

Change the Focus of the Conversation. This question changes the whole nature of the conversation. It is no longer "Will you listen to me?" but rather "How much are you capable of investing if I can fulfill the promise contained in my opening question?"

The prospect might say, "Yes, if the investment is as good as you say, I could invest five thousand today." You could further qualify the prospect by saying, "If you *really* liked it, could you invest ten thousand, or more?"

The prospect can say either yes or no. In either case, you are qualifying the prospect more narrowly and determining exactly what his financial situation is, even before you begin talking about your product or service.

Let's say the prospect says, "I don't think I have five thousand dollars."

You can then ask, "Well, could you invest three thousand if it was the best investment that you've ever seen?"

The prospect might then say, "Well, if it was as good as that, I could probably invest three thousand."

The Qualified Prospect. With these questions, you have qualified the prospect exactly in terms of his financial capacity. By answering your question, he is now giving you permission to give your presentation and to prove whether or not you have the best investment, or the best deal, or the best offer, or the best combinations of features and benefits, or the best of whatever it happens to be that you offered him in your opening question.

You can then give your presentation and demonstrate that what you are offering is absolutely excellent for him, right now, all things considered. At the end of your presentation, he cannot say that he can't afford it or that he doesn't have the money right now or that he has to talk it over with someone else. He has already agreed that, if your product or service is an excellent choice for him, he is in a position to buy it at this time.

It Works with Any Product. You can use this demonstration close to begin the sales process for virtually any product or service. You can use it to sell software and systems, business opportunities or financial investment advice, insurance or business services. If you are selling life insurance, for example, you could ask, "Mr. Prospect, if I could show you the most comprehensive insurance policy available to protect yourself, your family, and your home, at perhaps the lowest available price in the market today, would you be in a position to make a decision right now?"

When I was selling sales training to businesses, I would ask, "Mr. Prospect, if I could show you a way to increase your sales by 20 to 30 percent over the next six to twelve months, are you in a position to go ahead with it right now?"

If the prospect says, "Well, yes, if you can show me a way to increase my sales by 20 to 30 percent, I could make a decision immediately," your job is then to show the prospect that your product or service will definitely deliver on the promise you made in your opening statement.

You Can Demand an Answer. The beauty of the demonstration close is that it forces the prospect to give you an answer at the end of the presentation. Instead of saying that he needs to think about it or talk it over with someone else or check his finances, or some other excuse, he has promised to give you an answer immediately, one way or another.

Buyer Personality Types

There are six basic personality profiles that you will run into every day in selling. It is important that you recognize these different personality styles and that you learn how to deal effectively with each one.

1. The Apathetic Buyer

The first personality type you will meet in selling is the *apathetic* prospect. This type of buyer represents about 5 percent of the total. He is the kind of person who is never going to buy anything, no matter how good it is. He is usually pessimistic, cynical, and often depressed or uninterested.

The apathetic buyer doesn't care how good it is, how cheap it is, or how successful it is for other people. He's not going to buy, even if you give it away.

You run into apathetic buyers occasionally. They usually have a lot of problems in their own personal and business lives. They are down on themselves, down on life, and down on you. They have so many problems that they just don't care what you have to offer. Even if you are offering an apathetic buyer a one-hundred-dollar prize for five dollars, he wouldn't take it.

> **Even if you are offering an apathetic buyer a one-hundred-dollar prize for five dollars, he wouldn't take it.**

They waste your time. A friend of mine was once selling an excellent product for $295. The person with whom he was speaking was perfectly qualified to buy it and use it. He needed it, and he could afford it. But he was an apathetic buyer.

No matter what my friend said, this customer replied by saying, "It's too expensive; it's too expensive; it's too expensive."

Finally, in exasperation, the salesperson asked him, "What if I gave it to you for two hundred dollars?"

"It's still too expensive."

My salesman friend said, "How about one hundred?"

The apathetic buyer said, "I still couldn't afford it."

Finally, my friend said, "How about five dollars?"

"I still wouldn't buy it."

This is the typical apathetic buyer. They just don't care. They are negative and indifferent. When you meet these people, you will recognize them right away. Instead of tiring yourself out with them, extricate yourself as politely as you can and leave. Go and talk to someone else who will be more likely to buy.

2. The Self-Actualizing Buyer

On the other end of the scale of buyer types, you find the *self-actualizing* buyer. The self-actualizing buyer is exactly the opposite of the apathetic buyer. These buyers also represent about 5 percent of the customer market.

The self-actualizing buyer knows *exactly* what he wants, exactly the features and benefits he is seeking, and exactly what price he is willing to pay for it. If you have what he is looking for, he will take it immediately, right now, with few or no questions. He is positive, pleasant, and a pleasure to deal with. All you have to do is have the product or service he seeks, and the sale is made.

These buyers are rare. The self-actualizing buyer, like the apathetic buyer, is rare, never more than one in twenty prospects. But if you call on enough people, every so often you run into one of these self-actualizing buyers. And the sale is so easy that you say to yourself, *If I could sell like this all the time, I'd be rich!*

In dealing with self-actualizing buyers, always sell them exactly what they say they want. Don't try to sell them something else or something different, and don't change the specifications. You might give them some additional information, but don't try to talk them into something other than what they have their hearts set on. If you don't have what they want, tell them immediately that you don't have it and suggest to them where they might find it.

3. The Analytical Buyer

The third type is the *analytical buyer*. This person represents about 25 percent of the market. This type of buyer is self-contained and task-oriented. He is not particularly outgoing, but he is quite concerned about accuracy and detail. The primary motivator of the analyzer buyer is *accuracy*.

You will find these people in any field that requires detail orientation to be successful. They will be accountants, engineers, bankers, financiers, loan officers, and computer specialists. The primary focus of their questions to you will be the exact numbers, details, and specifications of what you sell.

Slow down and be exact. When you are dealing with an analytical buyer, you must slow down and avoid generalizations. Be specific and clear. Be prepared to prove, on paper, everything you say. The more precise you can be about the benefits of your product or service and how this customer can acquire them, the easier it is for this person to eventually make a buying decision.

The more detail you give him about how your product works, what it costs, how it performs, how it will be serviced, and so on, the happier he will be. These buyers love details. They can sit and study details, charts, and graphs for hours.

Analytical buyers do not make decisions in a hurry. They are *slow* to make up their minds. They need to be left alone with your material to reflect on and analyze it. They will often come back to you with a series of questions for clarification. There is no point in trying to rush these people. They are far more concerned about making the correct decision than they are about saving money or speeding up the transaction.

4. The Relater Buyer

Another type of customer you will deal with is the *relationship-oriented* person. These represent approximately 25 percent of the customer market, depending on what you sell. They tend to be self-contained and not particularly exuberant or expressive. You have to slow down and relax to get along well with them.

Relaters are very concerned about *people*. They are sensitive to how people think and feel about various subjects. In considering a product or service, they are concerned about how people might react or respond to their choices. They imagine what people's opinions might be, positive or negative, and they are often hypersensitive to the opinions of other people.

Relaters naturally gravitate toward the "helping" professions. They become teachers, personnel administrators, psychologists, nurses, and social workers.

They need to be liked. This type of customer worries about what people might think if the relater bought a particular product or service. She always has to talk it over with someone, often with lots of people. Sometimes she has to ask every member of her family, plus her friends and associates, before she can buy a new product or service.

The primary motivation of relaters is to *get along well with others*. They strive for harmony and happiness among the people around them and become distressed at the thought of someone being unhappy for any reason.

Focus on other happy customers. When you are selling a product or service to a relater, she will ask you a lot of questions about others who use the product. She will want to know if the product will be popular and accepted by the other people who will be affected by her purchase. She wants to be sure that others will find it attractive and suitable. If you are selling her a home, her primary concern will be the likely reactions of other people when they see and visit the home.

When you sell a relater clothes or cars, her main interest will be how other people respond to her choices.

Build a relationship. Relaters like to talk and ask questions about you and how you think and feel. They like to talk about the product or service and how other people have reacted to buying and using it. They want to develop a relationship with the salesperson until they feel comfortable talking about your product or service in the first place.

When you deal with a relater, or an emotional buyer, she may want to spend an hour or two getting to know you, and then have you come back and spend another hour or two to build the relationship. She wants to feel comfortable with you so that she can get her mind around you and the product or service you are offering.

Don't rush them. Relater-type buyers tend to be slow in making up their minds; they are generally hesitant and indecisive. They like to think about things a lot. They can decide to buy your product and then change their minds completely if one other person voices criticism or disapproval of their decision. You must develop the ability to be patient, sensitive, and thoughtful when dealing with relationship-oriented buyers.

5. The Driver Buyer

The fifth type of buyer is more task oriented than any other kind. He has the personality profile of the *director*. He is direct, impatient, and wants to get straight to the point. He is businesslike and practical. His greatest concern is *getting results.*

Because the task-focused buyer is impatient and outgoing, he will be direct and to the point with you. He will want to know what your product is, what it does, what results he will get, how much it costs, how sure he can be that your product or service will deliver on your promises, and how long it will take.

Get straight to the point. A driver buyer does not like small talk, and he has no interest in developing a warm relationship with the salesperson. He wants to get to the bottom line quickly and make a decision, *yes* or *no.*

Results- or task-focused persons gravitate to those occupations where this temperament is most in demand. They become entrepreneurs, hard-driving salespeople, and sales managers. They become senior executives in positions where they are directly responsible for measurable results. They are fire chiefs and the heads of SWAT teams. They are people who get the job done fast and do it well.

They are busy and preoccupied. Task-focused buyers are busy. You are interrupting them and keeping them away from something that they consider to be more important than you. They want you to cut to the chase quickly. They don't want a big buildup about how your product or service was conceived and designed. They only want you to answer the question, "What's in it for me?"

They only want you to answer the question, "What's in it for me?"

This type of buyer is a pleasure to deal with if you can demonstrate that your product or service will get him the results he wants. Like all buyers, he seeks improvement, and the clearer it is that your product or service will improve his life or work, the faster he will give you a yes answer.

Task-focused buyers are decisive and clear. They know what they want, and if you have it, they will want to get it and begin using it *immediately*. When you deal with a buyer like this, you must speed up your presentation, get to the bottom line quickly, and focus on the specific results or benefits that he will enjoy if he buys from you. This type of buyer represents about 25 percent of potential buyers, depending on what you sell.

6. The Socializer Buyer

The sixth type of buyer is the "socializer"-type buyer. This person is outgoing and extroverted. He likes working with and through people to get results. He is often called the "integrated buyer" in that he operates with a nice balance between people orientation and task orientation.

This type of buyer gravitates toward fields that require a high degree of coordination among different types of people to get the job done. They become supervisors, managers, and executives, as well as orchestra conductors, senior administrators in large professional firms, presidents of nonprofit organizations, and other positions where the ability to coordinate a variety of people to accomplish goals is necessary.

The socializer is achievement-oriented. Because of his extroverted, socializer-type nature, the chief concern of this person is himself and other people. He likes to talk about you as well as himself. He likes to talk about achievement and results. He enjoys telling you what he has done in the past and is very interested in knowing about you and what you have accomplished.

Sometimes the socializer buyer agrees too quickly and does not remember details. He might agree to do something with you or buy something from you, and a few days later, forget about it completely. Or even worse, he will remember the conversation differently and will be surprised at your interpretation of your meeting with him.

Put it on paper. When you deal with this kind of extroverted, outgoing buyer, as soon as you reach an agreement of any kind, you should write it down and get a copy off to him. Remember, with this type of buyer, "understandings prevent misunderstandings."

This type of buyer represents about 25 percent of the customer market. You can always tell when you meet a socializer-type buyer, because he will be warm, friendly, outgoing, interested in you, and will ask a lot of questions.

Different Strokes for Different Folks

Most successful salespeople tend to be either *socializers* or *directors*, or a combination of these two styles. A relater-type salesperson would usually be too sensitive to the opinions of others to ever ask for the order or try to close the sale. An analyzer-type salesperson would be so concerned about details and information gathering that he would never call on a prospect. If he did call on a prospect, he would be far too concerned about getting more information for the prospect than he would be in asking for the order.

The great problem in sales is that we all tend to see the world through our own eyes. As a result, we tend to treat everybody else as if they are the way we are. If you are a socializer, you will treat everyone else as if they are also socializers. If you are a director-type salesperson, you will be blunt and to the point and expect people to make quick decisions once you have shown them good reasons to buy.

Personality flexibility. To achieve success in sales, you must develop *personality flexibility.* This requires that you take a few moments to assess the type of prospect you are talking to and adjust your personality accordingly.

If you are talking to a *relater*, slow down, ask a lot of questions, and focus on the relationship. Take the time to help the prospect understand how your product or service will be appreciated and accepted by others who will be affected by it. Don't rush the person or try to get her to make a quick decision. By going slowly and patiently, you will eventually succeed with a relater-type buyer.

When dealing with an *analyzer*, again you must slow down and concentrate on details. Take time to answer every question, preferably in writing. Be specific with regard to your claims. In your conversation, allow silences and give the prospect an opportunity to think about what you have just said. Be patient, polite, and persistent.

Give the Customer What He Wants

In dealing with a director-type buyer, you must get straight to the point. Even if you are a socializer and you like to talk and get to know people, you must hold this tendency in check while dealing with a driver. Instead, answer his questions directly and focus on the bottom-line result he will get from using your product or service. The more convinced the driver is that your product or service will help him in a short period of time, the faster he will make a buying decision.

When dealing with a socializer, be positive and open. When the prospect begins talking about personal or business matters that have nothing to do with your product, gently bring the conversation back to focus on the reason for your visit. When the prospect agrees to go ahead, write the sale up quickly and get a signature as fast as you can. Otherwise, he might forget.

Take Time to Observe and Analyze Others

Before you begin to sell, figure out what type of person you are talking to, and then structure your answers and your presentation in such a way that it satisfies *their* needs rather than *yours*.

Even better, develop four separate sales presentations—the Analyzer/Thinker, the Relator/People person, the Director/Driver, and the Socializer/Achievement type of buyers. Be prepared to slip in and out of different sales roles as you find yourself dealing with different types of customers.

Moving Right Along

The true beginning of the sales process is *after* the salesperson has established a certain degree of trust and rapport with the prospect. *Trust* is the major factor in the sales process today. Until a person likes and trusts you, he is not open to what you are selling or how good it can be for him or his company. Trust is everything.

The bigger the product or service, the longer it usually takes to develop this feeling of trust and rapport. With large products or services, the entire first meeting can be taken up with feeling each other out and sensing whether or not there is a good fit between a salesperson and the company.

The Way to Build Trust

The very best way to build trust in a sales relationship is to *ask the prospect questions and listen carefully to the answers.* The more you show that you are genuinely interested in the prospect and his situation, the more the prospect will be open to giving you information and accepting your recommendations.

And never even start talking about your product or service until you have activated the *friendship factor.* You have to develop a bond of friendship before you can bridge into the development of a customer relationship.

Customers Are Careful

In selling expensive, sophisticated products with long life and installation time, it will often take three or four visits just to reach the point where the relationship is strong enough that you can talk business seriously. It is not uncommon for the sales process to require six months or more of meetings and proposals before the customer feels comfortable enough to make a large, long-term commitment. Be patient.

There is a good reason for this caution and delay. In many cases, the prospect's reputation and even career can be on the line. If he makes the wrong buying decision for his company, it can cost him his job. He can be demoted or even fired. For this reason, he cannot afford to make a mistake.

Begin Qualifying Early

Use the approach close or the demonstration close in your first inter-action with the customer. This enables you to qualify him immediately. The answer to one or both of these questions tells you at the beginning whether or not he is in the market for your product.

"If I could show you exactly the car you are looking for at perhaps the best price in the city, would you be interested in taking it for a drive?"

If the prospect says, "No, I just bought a car, and I won't need another one for a few years," then you know that this person is not a prospect. There is no point in trying to establish a high-quality relationship and understand more about her situation. She is not in the market.

The Purpose of the Presentation

Your opening question is to discover whether or not a person is a prospect for what you are selling. The purpose of subsequent questioning is to further qualify the prospect and to discover the key reasons why he might buy.

Each product contains a variety of features and benefits. "Features arouse interest, but benefits arouse buying desire" the saying goes.

The purpose of the presentation is to explain the features that your product or service includes and to demonstrate the benefits that they offer to your prospect. In a way, you are a bit of a detective. You are look-ing for clues that will lead you to the sale. You are presenting features and benefits for the purpose of eliciting buying interest on the part of the prospect. You are watching and listening to uncover reasons why he would buy.

Present One Feature/Benefit at a Time

The process of your presentation is not to show all of the information available on your product or service. It is to show one feature or one benefit at a time and to find out which of these benefits are of greatest interest to your prospect.

If you have ten features and benefits listed in order of descending importance, from the most attractive benefit your product offers down to the least, unveil your features and benefits in that order. If your prospect brightens up and becomes intensely interested when you mention your second most desirable benefit, you can then focus on that, and even start moving toward closing the sale.

Conclude the Sale

Once it is clear that your customer most desires a particular benefit that your product or service offers, you don't need to go through numbers three through ten. When you have found the *hot button,* begin focusing on that specific benefit, showing the customer how he can enjoy that benefit when he buys your product.

The prospect says, in response to a particular point in your presentation, "Wow! That's great. I've never seen that before. We need that around here. How long does it take to get something like that delivered?"

When this happens, you can ask for the order *immediately.* You don't need to go on talking any further. Simply say, "How soon would you need this?" and close the sale.

Buyers Are Sometimes Ready Now

One of the top mutual-funds salespeople I ever met had spent years developing his sales presentation. It moved from the general to the particular. It included every benefit that an investor could enjoy from a mutual fund. By the time the presentation was complete, it included thirty-two different points at which he could close the sale.

What he told me was that every prospect is either very close to buying when he meets the salesperson for the first time, or very far away. Actually, most prospects are somewhere in between. Some prospects only need one or two reasons to say yes. Other prospects require a much longer sales process before they are ready to buy. His sales presentation was designed to be effective with any prospect he met at any stage of the buying cycle.

Ask for the Order Early

Sometimes he could close right at the beginning with a highly qualified prospect. In his mutual fund presentation, he would start by asking a question such as, "Would you like to see a way to get the highest return on your money with the lowest possible risk in the market today?"

If the prospect said yes, my friend would take out a piece of paper and draw two circles. He would say, "Mr. Prospect, these two circles represent what you can do with your money. If you put your money into the first circle, into a traditional savings account, you can earn 3 to 5 percent on your money before taxes. Isn't that right?

"But if you put your money into the second circle, into a well-managed mutual fund, you can make 10 to 15 percent on your money and pay no taxes on the money until you withdraw it. Which of these two would you prefer?"

Often the prospect would say, "Well I would rather get 10 to 15 percent on my money."

The salesman would say, "Great! Why don't we get started right away?"

Take Action to Close the Sale

He would then take out an application form, write the date in the upper right-hand corner, and ask, "What is the correct spelling of your last name?" When the prospect gave him the spelling of his name, the sale was made. He would go on to wrap up the details and conclude the transaction. This salesman eventually became one of the most successful and highest-paid people in his field in the country.

Keep the Initiative

Sometimes the prospect would say, "Wait a minute, wait a minute. I need some time to think about this."

He would immediately say, "May I ask, how much money do you have in your savings account today?"

"About five thousand dollars."

My friend would then say, "Mr. Prospect, which do you think is best, 3 to 5 percent, or 10 to 15 percent?"

"Well, I guess 10 to 15 percent is better," his prospect would respond.

"Exactly! Do you have your checkbook with you?" He would then simply *assume the sale* and begin filling out the form. The prospect would have to stop him to keep the sale from going through. He seldom did.

What he found was that, in dealing with a qualified prospect, he could roll into the close of the sale as soon as the prospect made it clear that he wanted the primary benefit that he would get from buying the product. What we have found over the years is that many sales are delayed far longer than they need to be because salespeople are reluctant to ask for the order and bring the transaction to a close.

> **Many sales are delayed far longer than they need to be because salespeople are reluctant to ask for the order and bring the transaction to a close.**

Selling Tangibles Versus Intangibles

Closing the sale on a tangible product requires a different method than closing on an intangible product. When you have made a presentation on a tangible product, such as a car, a photocopier, a cellular telephone or a refrigerator, and the prospect has no further questions, you should ask for the order immediately. When the prospect fully understands what you are selling, how it works, and how he or she will benefit from owning and enjoying it, it is time to close the sale.

When you have completed your presentation, the prospect knows everything that he will ever know about buying and enjoying your product or service. He will not learn anything new or different after you leave or he leaves. This is the high point of the sales presentation. From this point onward, the customer will gradually forget the features and benefits of the product and gradually lose his interest and desire in purchasing.

Be Polite but Persistent

If the prospect says, "Well, it looks pretty good; let me think it over," you can immediately reply by saying, "Mr. Prospect, at this moment you already know everything you will ever know about this product. From what you've told me, it looks like it's an excellent choice for you. Why don't you just take it?"

You will be absolutely amazed at how often the prospect will say, "Well, OK. I'll take it."

But if you give the prospect an opportunity to walk away and "think it over" chances are the prospect will gradually forget why he was ever attracted to your product or service in the first place. Even worse, the prospect will run into another salesperson who is a little more assertive, and will end up buying your product from the other person. This happens all the time.

No More Callbacks

When I was a new salesman, just starting out, I was selling a discount card from office to office for about one hundred local restaurants. The price was twenty dollars. Whenever the owner of the card showed it in a restaurant, he would get 10 to 20 percent off the bill. The card would therefore pay for itself in one or two uses. It was a simple product, a simple benefit, a simple decision, and a simple sale.

But when I went out selling, I was really nervous. I would make my presentation and then wait. The prospect would invariably say, "Well, let me think it over."

I would thank the prospect very much and promise to call back on him in a few days after he had a chance to "think it over." Surprise, surprise! Nobody ever thought it over, and nobody bought the card. When I phoned, the prospect was never available. If I went back to his office, I was left sitting in the waiting room indefinitely. I was making almost no sales, and I was getting desperate.

The Light Went On

One day, I had a revelation. I realized that it was *me* who was causing prospects to hesitate from buying. I had already decided in the back of my mind that people needed to think it over. I would even suggest, if the prospect was hesitating, "Why don't you think it over?"

From that day forward, I developed a new tactic. After I had given my presentation and the prospect said, "Well, let me think it over," I would say, "I'm sorry. I don't make callbacks."

I remember the first time I said this to a prospect. He was surprised. He said, "What do you mean?" I told him, "Mr. Prospect, you know everything you need to know to make a decision today. This is a great product that pays for itself in one to two uses. After that you can save five or a hundred times the cost of the card. Why don't you just take it?"

To my surprise, the prospect said, "OK. That makes sense. I'll take it."

I walked out with a whole new attitude toward selling and closing. On my next call, I did and said the same things and again got a sale. On my third call, it was the same. Soon, I was selling more than anybody else in my company, and more than most of them put together. I sold to virtually every person I spoke to because I refused to make callbacks. Think about how this might apply to your selling as well.

Intangibles Are Different

If you are selling an *intangible* product, where the prospect may or may not be in a position to benefit from the values contained in your offering, you usually need to make more than one call.

On the first call, you merely separate *prospects* from *suspects*. You ask questions and qualify the prospect to determine whether or not he can benefit from what you sell. You find out his exact needs and then arrange to return for a second appointment with some recommendations and perhaps a written proposal.

Use the Sales "Two-Step"

In selling an intangible product, such as an insurance policy, an investment, or any kind of service that requires customizing and tailoring to the specific needs of the customer, use the *two-step sale*. On your first call, you ask questions to determine if the prospect can benefit from your product or service. On the second call, you return with a proposal or a recommendation, complete with prices and terms, and show the prospect how he or she can most benefit from what you are selling.

The reason you use a two-step sale when selling a more complex service is because you are not in a position to make a buying recommendation in the first call. You do not have enough information, nor do you have sufficient rapport and trust, to ask for the order.

Prior Planning Prevents Poor Presentations

One behavior that separates highly paid professionals from poorly paid amateurs in the sales profession is the *planned presentation*. The planned presentation is twenty times more powerful than the spontaneous presentation. All sales professionals in the top 10 percent use a planned presentation. The low money earners, those in the bottom 80 percent of salespeople, simply say whatever comes out of their mouths when they meet with customers. This is not the path for you.

> **Low money earners, those in the bottom 80 percent of salespeople, simply say whatever comes out of their mouths when they meet with customers. This is not the path for you.**

The planned presentation is a step-by-step process of *learning* and *teaching*. It begins with your opening question. From your opening question, you move through the process of learning the situation and needs of the prospect to teaching the prospect what your product does and what it can do for him. You move from the general to the particular, the known to the unknown.

Show, Tell, and Ask Questions

The simplest process is a "feature and benefit" presentation. A simple format you can use for every feature and benefit is the three parts—*show, tell,* and *ask questions.*

For example, if you were selling a new piece of computer software, you would *show* the prospect the software loaded onto the computer. You would then *tell* the prospect how the software can improve his business. Finally, *ask a question:* "Would this be helpful to you in your business?"

Three-Part Presenting

Another three-part method of presenting your product uses the structure: *"Because of this, you can, which means . . ."* These three parts are the product feature, the product benefit, and then the customer benefit, which is the real reason the customer will buy.

For example, if you were selling a flat-screen television that hangs on the wall, you could say, "Because of this flat screen [product feature], you can see from every angle [product benefit], which means that you can turn your living room into a theater for your family and friends [customer benefit].

List every feature and benefit of your product or service, and then write out both types of presentation. Show what it is, tell what it does, and then ask for feedback or approval. Explain the product feature, the benefit of that feature for the product, and then the benefit to the customer of both. You will be amazed at how much more persuasive your presentations become.

What Your Product Does

There are two different approaches to presenting any product or service, one used by the professionals and the second used by amateurs. The first approach, used by highly paid professionals, is to focus on what the product "does." The second approach, used by low-paid amateurs, is to focus on what the product "is."

In reality, all the customer cares about is what the product *does*, what's in it for him. In selling to businesses, the primary reason that anyone buys anything is to either make or save time or money. These are the answers to what your product or service "does." When you speak to businesspeople, they are only concerned with the end result, the direct, measurable outcome that they will get from giving you money for your product or service.

Four Questions You Must Answer

Businesspeople ask themselves four questions. You must answer these questions clearly and distinctly if you are going to make the sale. The questions are:

1. How much do I *pay?*

2. How much do I *get back?*

3. How *soon* do I get these results?

4. How *sure* can I be that I will get the results you promise?

Your entire sales presentation must revolve around answering these questions to the prospect's satisfaction.

Often, you will have to *build a case* for buying and using your product or service. Very much like a lawyer presenting a case in court, you will have to present one piece of evidence after the other, in sequence, with each feature and benefit leading to and reinforcing the next feature and benefit.

Emotion or Logic?

Sometimes I ask my audiences, "What percentage of a person's decisions is based on emotions, and what percentage is based on logic?"

Almost everyone will say that people are 90 percent emotional and only 10 percent logical. But the correct answer is that people are *100 percent emotional.* Thinking takes time and effort, but emotions are instantaneous. As I discussed earlier, this is why in sales, prospects *decide emotionally and then justify logically.*

If a prospect *feels good* about you and your company, if he likes you and respects you, if you have a good relationship, then the power of "liking" will very often lead to the sale.

Logic Makes Sales

Nonetheless, no matter how much the prospect wants your product emotionally, he still must be convinced logically that he will get the emotional benefits that he desires. As the saying goes, "Logic makes sales."

When you build your presentation from the ground up, moving from point to point, offering specific benefits and then explaining logically how the prospect achieves those benefits, your sales presentation is built on a solid foundation. Once the customer decides to buy, he will remain sold afterward, rather than having misgivings or buyer's remorse.

Here is an example of how I used to sell sales training, beginning with the emotion, the desire to increase sales results, and then reinforcing it with the logical reasons why this was achievable.

My opening question would be, "Mr. Prospect, would you be interested in seeing a way to increase your sales by 20 to 30 percent over the next six to twelve months?"

If the prospect was responsible for sales, and qualified, he would say, "Sure, what is it?"

I would respond, "Mr. Prospect, this is a proven methodology that has worked for hundreds of companies to increase their sales, and it is unconditionally guaranteed. If it doesn't work, it costs you nothing."

This would immediately relax the prospect and enable him to open up and listen to me with great interest.

Ask Logical Questions

"Mr. Prospect, who are your highest-paid salespeople? Are they the ones with the highest levels of motivation or the lowest levels of motivation?"

The prospect would always say, "My top people are the most motivated."

I would say, "Great, that's what everyone says. Let me tell you what I think is the best definition of motivation. It is this: 'motivation comes from an enhanced feeling of competence.'

"In other words, Mr. Prospect, people are the most motivated when they feel that they are most capable of getting results. Isn't that true?" The prospect would almost always agree.

"Mr. Prospect, what we have found is that the more you train your people with proven sales skills and techniques, the more motivated they are to use them to make more sales and more money for themselves. Does that make sense to you?"

Again, the prospect would almost always agree.

"Mr. Prospect, what we've found is that when we train people with these advanced selling skills, their sales go up immediately. More important, once they have these new skills, they can use them over and over to get even better results. And the more they use these skills, the better they get at them. Does that seem sensible?"

Give Measurable Benefits

"Mr. Prospect, if your average sales increased just 10 percent in the first month, they would probably continue to increase throughout the entire year. Isn't that right?"

Again, the prospect would agree.

"Mr. Prospect, if your sales went up steadily from the first month, throughout the entire year, they would easily increase 20 to 30 percent on average. How much would that mean in terms of total dollars to your bottom line if you increased your sales 20 to 30 percent over the next twelve months?"

The prospect would quickly calculate that his return on investment in sales training would easily be 1,000 percent or more. For every dollar he spent on sales training, he would get back ten dollars or more to his bottom line. Once the prospect had made this calculation, it was quite easy to close the sale.

Guarantee Satisfaction Whenever Possible

My closing argument would be, "Mr. Prospect, if anyone who takes this course does not feel that he or she will get a 10 or 20 percent increase in sales by using these ideas, there will be no charge for that person. If you personally do not feel that your people will get a 10 or 20 percent increase in sales by using these ideas, there will be no charge for the entire program. How does that sound?"

Using this presentation, going from the general to the particular, focusing on the benefit but emphasizing the logical, financial benefit for that prospect, I was able to sell *millions* of dollars' worth of sales training. And because the sales methods and techniques were so powerful and effective, there were never any requests for refunds or rebates. You can design your sales presentation so that it achieves the same kinds of results.

Price Comes Last

Interestingly enough, it was only when I had closed the sale and gotten an agreement to conduct our sales training program that the prospect would suddenly become alert and ask, "Wait a minute. How much is this going to cost?"

When you have designed and given your sales presentation effectively, the question of price will only come up at the end, after the decision to buy has been made. In fact, if the prospect asks you how much it is going to cost before you have finished showing him what he will get and what your product or service will do for him, refuse to give the price. Put off the question. Say, "That is a good question; I'm going to get to that in a moment."

Here's a wise proverb from the world of sales: "Price out of place kills the sale." If you give the price too early, before the customer knows what the price is for, he will often become preoccupied with the amount you are going to charge rather than the benefits he is going to receive. Always delay discussion of pricing until the end of the presentation, when the prospect clearly wants to enjoy the benefits that your product or service offers.

Learning and Teaching Continually

In a good presentation, during the process of learning and teaching, you learn what the prospect needs and you teach him how he will get it from the product or service that you are selling.

As you go through your sales presentation, asking questions and inviting feedback, you learn more and more about what the prospect really wants. When your presentation is well planned, it has an irresistible logic and flow. When you reach the end of your presentation, the prospect should be ready to buy what you are selling. This is why the real close takes place in the presentation.

When you have made a good presentation, and the prospect is convinced that your product is going to give him benefits that far outweigh the costs, then it is simply a matter of wrapping up the details at the end of the presentation.

Take the Time to Be Perfectly Clear

Before you can begin your sales presentation, you must be absolutely clear about the specific needs of this particular prospect and how your product or service can satisfy those needs. In this qualification phase, the very best way to elicit these needs is by asking planned, open-ended questions that elicit specific information.

Listening is the key to building trust, to learning the true needs of the prospect. It is also the key to establishing a high-quality relationship. In fact, listening is the key to sales success.

One of the greatest needs that each person has is to feel important, to be appreciated and esteemed by other people. Listening has been called "white magic" because of its enormous impact on influencing the emotions and personality of the other person.

Become a Great Listener

There are five keys to effective listening. You could attend every course, read every magazine article, and watch every video on listening, and they will still boil down to these five keys.

1. Listen Attentively

First, listen attentively, without interruptions. Listen without any attempt to leap in and share your own ideas.

Face the prospect directly. Lean forward. Nod, smile, and agree. Be an active listener rather than a passive listener. Focus on the mouth and eyes of the prospect when he is speaking.

Here is a good exercise. Imagine that your eyes are *sun lamps* and you want to give your prospect's face a *tan*. As you listen, keep moving your eyes up and down over your prospect's face, hanging on every word, as if she were about to give you the winning lottery number and she would only give it to you once.

> **Imagine that your eyes are sun lamps and you want to give your prospect's face a tan.**

Listen as though you have all the time in the world. Listen as if you would still be here if she wanted to talk for eight years, and you would love to hear every single word she says.

Listening Affects People. When a prospect is intensely listened to, he experiences specific physiological changes. His heart rate goes up. His blood pressure goes up. His galvanic skin response increases. Most importantly, when a person is intensely listened to, his *self-esteem* goes up. He feels more valued. He likes himself more, and as a result, he likes the person who is listening to him so intently.

Listening is the most powerful of all techniques in selling. All of the highest-paid sales professionals are described as "very good listeners." They "seek first to understand, then to be understood." They concentrate all of their attention on understanding the thoughts, feelings, and needs of the customer before they make any attempt to sell.

2. Pause Before Replying

Second, pause before replying or continuing. When the prospect finishes speaking, pause and wait for *three to five seconds* before you answer. Even if the prospect has asked you a question to which you know the answer, you must still discipline yourself to pause for a few moments.

There are *three* benefits to pausing. First, when you pause, you convey to the prospect that you are *carefully considering* what he just said. This tells him that you value him and his words. What he has said is too important for you to respond too quickly. As a result, you raise his self-esteem and self-respect. You make him feel better about himself, and by extension, better about you.

The second benefit of pausing is that it allows you to *hear the prospect* at a deeper level of mind. It's almost as though words soak into your mind as water soaks into the soil. When you allow silence after the prospect's words, you actually understand what he or she really meant, much more than you would if you replied immediately.

The third benefit of pausing before replying is that you avoid the *risk of interrupting* the prospect if he is just reorganizing his thoughts and preparing to begin speaking again.

Allow Silence in the Conversation. Salespeople must become comfortable with silence. This is critical to selling success. Most salespeople are a bit impatient, sometimes nervous, and eager to make the sale. As a result, they feel that they have to say something, anything, when a silence develops during the sales conversation.

Remember the saying, *the selling takes place with the* words, *but the buying takes place in the* silence.

Customers need time to process the sales conversation. If you do not allow silence, which permits what is being said to soak into their minds, they cannot process your sales message. At the end of your time together, they will have no choice but to say, "Leave it with me; let me think it over." And when they say this, you have in all likelihood lost the sale completely.

3. Question for Clarification

Third, question for clarification. Never assume that you know what the prospect really meant by what he just said. Instead, pause and then ask the question, *"How do you mean?"*

This is one of the great, all-purpose questions for sales success. No matter what the prospect says or no matter what his objection, you can always follow it up with "How do you mean?"

"It costs too much." How do you mean?

"We can't afford it." How do you mean?

"We are happy with our existing supplier." How do you mean?

"We don't have it in the budget." How do you mean?

Each time you ask the question, "How do you mean?" the prospect will *expand* on what he just said. He will give you more detail. And each elaboration increases the likelihood that he will tell you what you need to know to help him make a buying decision.

Questions Equal Control. Let me repeat this all-important principle in selling and communication: *the person who asks questions has control.* People are conditioned to respond to questions from early infancy. When you ask a person a question, he or she almost automatically gives you an answer.

When you are talking at about 100 to 150 words per minute, the prospect can process words at the rate of 600 words per minute. This means that the prospect has three-quarters of his time available to think of something else while you are speaking. Very often, prospects drift off into their own thoughts because they have so much thinking time available to them when you are giving your presentation.

But when you *ask a question*, 100 percent of the prospect's attention will be focused on answering you. It is almost as if you grabbed the prospect by the lapels and jerked him toward you. When you ask a question, the prospect cannot think of anything else but the answer until it is given, giving you the control.

4. Paraphrase It in Your Own Words

Feed back what the prospect just said in your own words. Paraphrase the prospect's comments or questions. This is known as the "acid test" of listening. When you can feed back what a customer says, you prove to the customer that you were *really* paying attention. You were not just like one of those toy dogs in the back of a car window with its head nodding up and down. You were really listening.

Only after you have listened attentively, paused before replying, questioned for clarification, and fed it back in your own words are you in a position to comment intelligently or to make a sales presentation.

Listening builds trust, and the very best way to get an opportunity to listen is to control the conversation with questions.

5. Use Open-Ended Questions

Earlier we covered the use of open-ended questions. These are questions that cannot be answered with yes or no. Whenever you ask a question beginning with the pronouns or adverbs *who, why, where, when, how, what,* and *which,* you encourage the prospect to talk and give you more information that can help you to make the sale.

Closed-Ended Questions

Use *closed-ended* questions to bring a conversation to a conclusion. These are questions that can *only* be answered with yes or a no. Closed-ended questions always begin with verbs, such as *are, is,* and *do.* "Are you ready to make a decision today? Is this what you are looking for? Do you want to get started right away?"

Remember to design your sales presentation around questions that you have planned in advance. As you have already learned, *telling* is not *selling*.

Presentation Methods

Your presentation should always move from the general to the particular in a logical order. Use what is called the "ascending close." With this, you present your product features and benefits in the order of importance, from the most to the least. Usually your most powerful benefit will arouse buying desire. But this is not always the case. Be prepared to walk through your features and benefits, remaining alert and aware of the prospect's reactions. Sometimes your third or fourth benefit will be what interests your prospect more than anything else.

Get the Prospect Involved

Get the prospect involved and keep him involved. Cause him to move. A prospect who is sitting there like a lump of stone, neither reacting nor responding, is not likely to buy when you have finished your presentation.

The very best salespeople are active in the sales conversation. Not only do they talk, but they move, use their faces, and gesture with their hands. They pass the prospect information and take it back. They ask him to calculate numbers and percentages.

Ask the Prospect to Sit Somewhere Else

Don't be afraid to pull your chair around the prospect's desk and sit next to him while making your presentation. Even better, get the prospect to move to a table or to another office where there is more room for your materials as you present your product. The more a prospect talks and moves in a sales presentation, the more likely it is that he will agree to buy at the end of your presentation.

> The more a prospect talks and moves in a sales presentation, the more likely it is that he will agree to buy at the end of your presentation.

Use Visual Aids to Sell

Use visual sales aids whenever possible. There are twenty-two times the number of nerves from the eye to the brain as from the ear to the brain. If all you are doing is talking, the prospect will have a hard time paying attention or remembering anything that you say.

Use pictures, graphs, illustrations, and even financial comparisons on paper to reinforce and drive home your key points.

The average attention span of an adult is about three sentences. Once you have spoken three sentences in a row without asking a question, showing a picture, or giving an illustration, the prospect becomes lost in his own world. He will be busy thinking about what he will do when you leave.

But as soon as you ask a question, you jerk the prospect awake and force him to focus his entire attention on your presentation. When you use illustrations combined with questions, you keep the prospect totally involved throughout your presentation.

Telling Is Not Selling

There's that adage again. That's because your most effective way of presenting is by taking every important piece of information that you have to convey and rephrasing it as a question. Instead of saying, "This costs

$295 per person," say, "Do you have any idea how much something like this normally costs per person?" Once you have asked it as a question, you will have the prospect's complete attention when you answer.

The Trial Close

Begin using the trial close very early in the presentation. It is one of the most powerful of all closing techniques, and it can be used throughout your selling work. Sometimes it is called the *signpost close* or the *check close*. You use it to find out if you are on the right track or to check if what you are talking about is important to the prospect. It is a wonderful way to get feedback continually throughout the presentation.

The beauty of the trial close is that it can be answered with a no without stopping the presentation.

You: "Do you like this color?"

Prospect: "No, I hate it; it's the worst color I've ever seen."

You: "No problem, we've got lots of other colors you would like better."

Ask for Feedback

Some of the most popular trial closing questions that you can ask are:

- Does this make sense to you so far?"
- Is this what you had in mind?"
- Do you like what I've shown you up to now?"
- "Would this be an improvement on your current situation?"
- "Are we right so far?"
- "This new photocopier will produce 150 copies a minute versus the standard of 100 copies per minute. Would this be important to you in your business?"

"No, I don't think so. We never need to produce a large number of copies in a short period of time."

"No problem, this machine has several other features that I think you will really like." And then you go on with the presentation.

Feedback Is Essential

When the prospect says no to a particular feature or benefit, he is giving you valuable feedback. He is not saying no to the entire offer. He is only saying no to that particular feature.

The difference between experienced salespeople and inexperienced salespeople in this area is that experienced salespeople present one feature or benefit and then ask for feedback. They make sure that they understand what the customer is thinking at each state of the sales presentation.

Inexperienced salespeople, out of nervousness, present every feature and benefit, one after another, without hesitating or stopping to get feedback. At the end of the presentation, the customer has gone into overload and has no choice but to say, "Leave it with me; let me think it over."

The Power-of-Suggestion Close

You can use the power-of-suggestion close throughout the presentation to plant seeds of readiness in the customer's mind. People think and make buying decisions largely based on stories and word pictures. People take in information in a logical form, but your brain can only hold a certain amount of data. However, your brain can hold millions of pictures and stories.

The very best salespeople are those who continually paint *emotional word pictures* about their product. Word pictures create images in the customer's mind. These images often trigger emotions such as buying desire. Long after the presentation, the prospect will forget all the facts you gave, but will still remember clearly the pictures and stories.

Create Word Pictures

For example, imagine that you are selling a car. You can say, "You are really going to love the way this car handles in the mountains."

What happens when you say this? The prospect sees and thinks of the car driving through the mountains. He or she instantly transports into driving this car around curves with forests and lakes on either side.

If you are selling homes, you could say, "You are really going to enjoy living on such a quiet street. It is just beautiful here. There is not a sound in the evenings. It's so relaxing."

When you describe a house like this, the individual immediately reaches out mentally and emotionally for the benefits. When his friends later ask why he bought this particular house, he will almost invariably talk about the house in terms of how quiet the neighborhood is.

Double Your Responses

When I was working as a sales consultant for a residential real estate company, we developed a powerful telephone question that doubled the number of people coming in to look at houses.

In the business of residential real estate, companies place advertisements in the newspapers for homes for sale, inviting prospective buyers to phone for more information. In most cases, prospective buyers will telephone, ask for the very best price and terms available for that house, and then hang up. Too often, the real estate company won't even get a chance to meet and talk to these people.

Answer Questions with Questions

Rather than giving facts and details on the home, we taught them to answer inquiries with a simple question. "Thank you for calling. May I ask you a question; are you looking for an ideal home in a quiet neighborhood?"

This question was carefully formulated. When the person answering the phone asked this question, it immediately triggered two mental pictures in the mind of the prospective buyer. The first mental picture was his or her personal definition of "an ideal home." This picture is different for every person. But the three words instantly caused the caller to visualize what he or she personally considered to be an ideal home.

The second picture this question triggered was the scene of a quiet neighborhood. The two pictures in combination invariably elicited the answer, "Of course. Do you have something that fits that description?"

The real estate agent would say, "Well, as a matter of fact, we have two houses that have just been listed that you might like to see. They aren't even in the newspapers yet. When would you have time to take a look at them?"

This simple approach, using the power-of-suggestion close, more than doubled the flow of prospects coming through this real estate office. Once prospects had come in and gone out to visit homes with one of the real estate agents, they typically stayed with that agent until they had found the type of home they were looking for.

Talking Past the Sale Close

In conjunction with the power-of-suggestion close, you can use the *talking past the sale close*. This method is very simple. You talk to the prospect as if he has *already* bought the product or service. You don't even ask him for a buying decision. You simply talk about how much he is going to enjoy the product or service now that he owns it.

For example, the prospect is considering retaining the services of your company. You say, "You are going to love the type of service that you get from our company. When you place an order, it's confirmed within thirty minutes and out within three days, faster than any other company in the business."

This immediately creates a mental picture of speed and efficiency in the customer's mind. The customer projects himself into the person of a satisfied customer, and sees himself enjoying the benefits you just described.

"You are going to adore living in this neighborhood. Even though it's quiet and peaceful, it's close to schools, shopping, and the freeway to get to work. This is a good choice!"

"With this photocopier in your office, it will sit over there in your staff room producing a hundred copies a minute, and it will be so quiet that you won't even know it's on."

In every case, prospects become customers when they have clear, exciting, emotional word pictures of themselves enjoying the benefits of the product or service that you are selling. Your job is to create as many exciting pictures as possible of the customer benefiting from what you sell. The more of these pictures you can create, the more irresistible your offer becomes.

> **Your job is to create as many exciting pictures as possible of the customer benefiting from what you sell.**

Top Sales Strategy

One of my graduates is a top salesperson for a recreational vehicle dealership. She sells RVs that cost as much as $500,000 each. She outsells her competitors, both at her own dealership and throughout the state, by three to five times. She is a superstar in her field. And she has a simple technique to achieve this goal.

When a couple comes in to look at a recreational vehicle, she first qualifies them to determine that they are serious buyers. She then shows them several vehicles to determine what size and price range they are interested in. Finally, she arranges to take them out for a combination lunch and test drive in the vehicle that they seem to like the most.

A couple of days later, as prearranged, she arrives at their home driving the vehicle. She has them make themselves comfortable inside, and then she drives them to an idyllic spot in a park, overlooking the lake, with the mountains in the distance. She swings the vehicle around so that this beautiful scene is facing the couple as they sit at the kitchen table. She then takes out a picnic basket, lays out a beautiful luncheon, and serves it to them as they sit looking at the mountains.

After lunch and after answering all their questions, she says, "Isn't this a beautiful way to live? Wouldn't you just love to be able to get away in this vehicle anytime you wanted?"

The couple looks at her, looks at each other, looks out over the mountains and the lake, and the decision is made. She sells more recreational vehicles than anyone else in her industry, and for good reason.

ACTION EXERCISES

1. Plan every sales presentation in advance; design it so that it moves from the general to the particular, from the known to the unknown, starting with your most attractive benefit.

2. Ask trial closing questions throughout; invite feedback and responses after every feature or benefit.

3. Take the time to determine the buyer personality style of the prospect you are talking to; make note of the questions he/she asks; these are good indicators.

4. Practice flexibility with your prospects and customers; speed up or slow down, be general or specific, so that you can sell to more diverse people.

5. Create emotional mental pictures of how happy your prospect will be while owning and using your product or service.

6. Design each part of your presentation to show, tell, and ask questions about each feature and benefit you present; keep the prospect involved and active.

7. Become an excellent listener; ask good questions, listen without interrupting, pause before replying, and feed it back in your own words to prove that you fully understand the prospect's situation.

The only certain means of success is to render more and better service than is expected of you, no matter what your task may be.

—OG MANDINO

8

10 KEYS TO SUCCESS IN SELLING

Be true to the best you know. This is your high ideal. If you do your best, you cannot do more.
—H. W. Dresser

The top 20 percent of salespeople earn 80 percent of the money. The top 5 percent or 10 percent of salespeople earn vastly more than that. Your goal is to become one of the very best and highest-paid people in your profession. Fortunately, this is easier than you might think.

Success Is Predictable

One of the turning points in my life was when I learned about the law of cause and effect. This law says that for every effect, such as high income, there is a specific cause, or causes. If you do what other successful people do, you will eventually get the same results that they do.

In the remaining pages, I would like to pass on to you some of the causes, or reasons, for great success. The more of them you practice, the better results you will get. Once you learn these ideas, you can practice them time and again. The more you practice them, the less effort will be required for optimum results. You will move onto the fast track in your sales career.

1. Do What You Love to Do

All truly successful, highly paid people, including salespeople, love what they do. You must learn to love your work and then commit yourself to becoming excellent in your field. These two go together, like a hand in a glove.

Invest whatever amount of time is necessary; pay any price; go any distance, make any sacrifice to become the very best at what you do. Commit to excellence. Join the top 10 percent.

Excellence Is a Decision. Sadly enough, the majority of people will often spend their entire lives in selling, and it will never occur to them that they should commit themselves to becoming excellent in doing it.

The good news is that you do not have to be the best in the world to live an extraordinary life. Success in sales goes to the person who is just a little better in the critical areas of selling. If you take the time and make the effort, if you really put your whole heart into what you are doing and learn to love the profession of selling, you will move into the big-money ranks of sales professionals.

Self-Esteem and Success. We spoke earlier about the importance of self-esteem and success. Psychologists have discovered that you can never really feel happy about yourself until you know that you are good at what you do. You can never genuinely like yourself and accept yourself as a worthwhile person until you have become very good in your chosen field.

The reason many people are unhappy is because when they wake up in the morning and look at themselves in the mirror, the person who looks back at them is not very good at anything that makes much of a difference. Men especially get their sense of self-worth from knowing that they are competent in their fields. If a man is not particularly good at what he does and is not recognized by others for his competence and ability, he feels unhappy and unfulfilled.

You Can Be the Best. Every single person has the ability to be good at something. Everyone has the ability to excel. It is almost as though nature has built an "excellence gene" into each person. And it is up to each person to discover what his or her area of excellence is, and then to put his or her whole heart into becoming really good in that area.

Michael Jordan was once complimented on his skills as a basketball player. The journalist said to him, "You were lucky to be born with such tremendous athletic ability."

Jordan replied, "Everybody has ability; but talent takes hard work."

Many people make the mistake of thinking that if they have the ability to excel in a field, it will come naturally. But the fact is that excellence is the result of years of hard, dedicated effort in a single direction. There is no substitute for hard work.

2. Decide Exactly What You Want

Don't be wishy-washy or vague. Decide exactly what it is you want in life. Set it as a goal and then determine what price you are going to have to pay to get it. Most people never do this.

According to the research, only about 3 percent of adults have written goals. And these are the most successful and highest-paid people in every field. They are the movers and shakers, the creators and innovators, the top salespeople and entrepreneurs. Almost everyone works for them.

> Only about 3 percent of adults have written goals. And these are the most successful and highest-paid people in every field.

The Goals Formula

Here is a simple seven-step formula for setting and achieving goals. I teach it everywhere I go, and it has often been life changing for my seminar participants.

First, decide *exactly* what you want. If you want to increase your income, be specific about the exact amount that you want to earn.

Second, write it down. A goal that is not in writing is merely a fantasy. It has no power or energy behind it. It is like a cartridge with no powder or like cigarette smoke in the air.

Third, set a deadline on your goal. Your subconscious mind loves deadlines. It requires a "forcing system" to activate all its powers.

If it is a large enough goal, set *subdeadlines.* If it is a ten-year goal, set a goal for each year, and then for each month of the coming year. Continually measure your progress against your goal and your deadlines.

Fourth, make a list of everything you can think of that you can possibly do to achieve your goal. When you think of new activities, add them to your list. Keep working at it until your list is complete.

The more individual steps you write down on your list, the more excited you become about achieving your goal and the more motivated you will be. Henry Ford said, "Any goal, no matter how large, can be achieved if you break it down into enough small steps."

Fifth, organize the list by sequence and priority. When you organize by sequence, you decide what has to be done before something else has to be done. You determine what comes first, what comes second, and so on.

When you organize by *priority,* you determine the most important item on your list, and then the second most important, then the third, fourth, and so forth.

Once you have a list of steps, organized by sequence and priority, you have a *plan.* A person with a goal and a plan will run circles around a person with only a wish and a hope.

Sixth, take action on your goal, whatever it is. The primary reason that people succeed greatly is because they are *action oriented.* The primary reason that people fail is because they do not take action. Failures always have an excuse to procrastinate, until finally their energy and desire are gone and they are back to where they started.

Seventh, do something *every day* that moves you toward your most important goal, whatever it is at that time. Do this 365 days per year. Develop the discipline of working on your goals daily so that it is as normal and as natural to you as breathing in and breathing out.

Set 10 Goals Immediately

Here is an exercise for you. Take a sheet of paper and write the word *Goals* at the top of the page, plus today's date. Then write down ten goals that you would like to achieve in the next twelve months. Write as quickly as possible. This exercise should only take you three to five minutes.

Once you have your list of ten goals, go over the list and ask yourself, *Which* one *goal on this list, if I were to achieve it within twenty-four hours, would have the greatest positive impact on my life?"*

The answer to that question becomes your *major definite purpose.* This becomes the organizing principle or focal point for your life.

Transfer this goal to the top of a clean sheet of paper and write it out clearly and in detail; make it *measurable.*

Set a deadline for when you intend to achieve it.

Make a list of everything you can think of that you will have to do to accomplish the goal.

Organize this list by sequence and priority into a plan.

Take action on this goal, and then *do* something *every day* until you achieve it.

Your Major Definite Purpose

When you get up in the morning, think about this goal. As you work through the day, think about this goal. Discuss this goal with the important people in your life. In the evening, before you go to sleep, think about this goal and what it will look like when you achieve it. Continually visualize your goal as if it were already a reality. Resolve in advance that you will never quit until you achieve this goal. *Failure is not an alternative!*

Change Your Life

This exercise will change your life. If you have the discipline and determination to follow all the steps listed above, within one year, and perhaps sooner, your entire life will be different. Both your sales and your income will increase dramatically. You will feel terrific about yourself. You will start to make rapid progress in every area of your life. You will attract people and circumstances into your life that can help you. Miracles will happen.

At the end of a year, you will look back and be speechless at what has happened over the past twelve months. All it takes is a pad of paper, yourself, and less than ten minutes. Give it a try. Write down ten goals, select one, make a plan, and see what happens.

3. Back Your Goal with Persistence and Determination

Once you begin, refuse to even consider the possibility of failure. Back your goal with perseverance and indomitable willpower. Decide to throw your whole heart and soul into your success and into achieving that goal.

Don't hold anything back. Make a complete commitment. Resolve that nothing will stop you or discourage you.

You can tell where you are going to be in one, two, or three years by how well you respond to the inevitable adversities, objections, and disappointments that you experience each day. Your level of persistence in the face of setbacks is your measure of your *belief* in yourself.

The Greek philosopher Epictetus once said, "Circumstances do not make the man; they simply reveal him to himself."

Adversity shows you what you are made of. As my friend Charlie Jones says, "It's not how far you fall, but how high you bounce, that counts."

You can always tell how successful you are going to be by how quickly you bounce back. Your degree of resilience is the mark and measure of your character. Your ability to take the hard work and rough shocks of selling, and to keep on keeping on, is the ultimate determinant of your success.

4. Commit to Lifelong Learning

Your mind is your most precious asset, and the quality of your thinking determines the quality of your life. Commit yourself to lifelong learning. I cannot emphasize this too often.

Not long ago, a college student sent out a thirty-nine-point questionnaire to all the presidents of Fortune 500 companies. Eighty-three of those presidents completed the questionnaire and sent it back. This is an extraordinary number of responses from such a busy group of people.

The student went through the questionnaires to find out what these business leaders considered to be the reasons for their success. Perhaps the most common piece of advice from these top people, repeated over and over again, was, "Never stop learning and getting better." This applies to you as well.

Your Mind Can Appreciate in Value. Read, listen to audio programs, attend seminars and courses, and never forget that the most valuable asset you will ever have is your mind.

But your mind can be made to *appreciate* in value. If you purchase a car, it begins to depreciate, to lose its value as soon as you drive it off the dealer's lot. If you buy any kind of physical object, it begins to deteriorate immediately. You can *increase* the value of your mind by continually feeding it new information that you can use to get better results.

Increase Your Value. Each person starts off in life with a limited amount of practical knowledge that he can use for the benefit of other people. As you learn, you become more valuable. The more knowledge you acquire that can be applied to practical purposes, the greater will be your rewards and the more you will be paid.

As you go through life, gaining additional experience, reading more books, and upgrading your skills, your knowledge grows and your rewards in life *increase*. As you move forward in the line of life, toward the success that is possible for you, the law of cause and effect applies.

In success, the law of cause and effect is summarized by "learn and do." Every time you learn and practice something new, you move ahead in the line. When you stop learning and doing, you stop moving forward. When you once more start learning and applying what you've learned, you start moving forward again. The more you learn and do, the faster you move toward the front of the line.

Keep Filling Your Bucket. Imagine that your current quantity of knowledge and skill is like water in a bucket. The water level determines your income. When you start off in life, your bucket has very little knowledge and skill in it. Your results and rewards are minimal as well. As you increase your level of knowledge and skill, your bucket gets fuller. Your level of rewards and recognition increases. Over the years, your bucket gets fuller, this level increases, and your income goes up.

But here's the problem. There is a hole in this bucket. If at any time you stop learning and practicing new skills or adding new knowledge and ideas, you do not stay in the same place. Your "water level" drops. You actually begin to fall back in the line of life. People start to pass you. If you do not continually upgrade your knowledge and skill, you lose your edge. Your current knowledge and skill become increasingly obsolete and of less value.

Never Stop Learning. An enormous number of adults do not understand this. They get their basic education, but then they try to coast on their minimal knowledge and skill for many years. They are flabbergasted and angry when younger people pass them in the race. They become frustrated. No one has ever told them that continuous learning is as essential as bathing or brushing their teeth each day. If you don't do it for any period of time, it soon becomes evident to everyone around you.

If you are not continually learning and growing, the knowledge you have is actually diminishing. The incompetent person of tomorrow is the person who has stopped learning today. The illiterate person is the person who is no longer learning, growing, and increasing his value every single day. The person who does not read is no better than the person who cannot read.

Resolve that you are going to learn and practice something new each day. Read every morning, listen to audio programs in your car, take all the training you can get, and continually put your new knowledge into action.

5. Use Your Time Well

Your time is all you have to sell. It is your primary asset. How you use your time determines your standard of living. Resolve therefore to use your time well.

> **Your time is all you have to sell. It is your primary asset.**

Because of the 80/20 rule, some things you do are worth vastly more than other things, even though they take the same number of minutes and hours. Your goal is to focus on those activities that contribute the very most value to your life and your work.

Begin every day with a list. The best time to make up your work list is the night before, prior to wrapping up for the day. Write down everything that you have to do the next day, starting with your fixed appointments and then moving on to everything you can think of. Never work without a list.

Time management experts say that you will increase your productivity by 25 percent, or gain two extra hours per day, by the very act of planning your day in advance. Your list becomes the key to your time and life management system.

Set Clear Priorities

Once you have a list, set priorities on your list. Determine what is more important and what is less important. Ask yourself, *If I could only do one thing on this list before I was called out of town for a month, which one thing would it be?*

Whatever your answer, put a circle around that item. Then ask yourself, *If I could only do two things on this list before being called out of town for a month, what would the second item be?"*

Circle that item as well. Then ask yourself this question one more time.

This exercise forces you to think about what is really important, rather than what is merely urgent or busywork. Once you have determined your highest priority task, you know where to start and what to work on.

Select Your Most Important Task

A good time management question for you to ask is, *what one thing, if done in an excellent fashion, would have the greatest positive impact on my work?* There is always one thing that you can do that, if you do it well, can have a significant influence on your results and your rewards.

A variation of this question is, *what can I, and only I, do that, if done well, will make a real difference?*

Every hour of every day, there is only one answer to this question. There is something that only you can do that will make a real difference. This is something that no one else will do for you, if you don't do it. But if you do it, and you do it well, it can make a real difference. What is it?

The final question you ask in setting priorities is, *what is the most valuable use of my time, right now?*

Again, ask this question every hour. There is always a single answer to this question. Your job is to make sure that, whatever you are doing, it is the most valuable use of your time at that moment.

Focus and Concentrate

The final key to time management, once you have made a list and set priorities, is for you to begin on the most important task before you, and then to concentrate on it fervently until it is complete. Your ability to focus and concentrate, to be absolutely clear about your most important task, and then to do only that task until it is done, will do more to double and triple your productivity and performance than anything else.

6. Follow the Leaders

Do what successful people do. Follow the leaders, not the followers. Do what the top people in your field do. Imitate the ones who are going somewhere with their lives. Follow the people who are achieving the kind of things that you want to achieve sometime in the future.

Look around you. Who are the people that you admire the most? Which ones are getting the results that you want to achieve in the months and years ahead? Identify the very best people in your field and pattern yourself after them. Decide to *be* like them. Associate with them as much as possible.

If you want to know how to be a successful salesperson, go to the top people in your business and ask them for advice. Ask them what books you should read and what audio programs you should listen to. Ask them what courses you should take. Inquire about their attitudes, philosophies, and approaches to their work and their customers.

Learn from the Best

Successful people will always help other people to be successful. People who are extremely busy with their own lives and work will always find time to help you, if you genuinely want to be successful.

When you ask for advice from a successful person, take that advice. Do what the winner encourages you to do. Buy the book and read it. Get the audio program and listen to it. Attend the course, and practice what you learn. Then go back to that person and tell him or her what you have done. That individual will want to help you even more.

Choose Your Role Models

At a seminar for more than a thousand sales professionals not long ago, a salesman came up to me at the break and told me an interesting story. I knew immediately that he was successful because of his appearance. He was well dressed, well-groomed, confident, positive, relaxed, and easygoing. He had the feeling of success about him.

He told me that when he started out, he hung around with the junior salespeople. Over his first six months, he noticed that there were four top salespeople in his company who seemed to associate mostly among themselves. They did not spend time with the junior salespeople.

He observed the junior salespeople, himself, and the top salespeople, and noticed one thing immediately. The higher-paid salespeople were dressed far better than the lower-paid salespeople. They were sharp, chic, and professional looking. They looked like successful people.

Ask for Advice

One day, he asked one of the top salespeople what he could do to be more successful. The salesperson asked him if he used a time management system. As it happened, this young fellow had never been introduced to a time management system. The successful salesperson told him the system he used and showed him where to get it. And he did. And he used it. And he began to use his time more efficiently.

After that, he began to model himself after the top salespeople. Not only did he ask them for advice about what to read and listen to, but he observed them and made them his role models. Each morning, before he started out, he would stand in front of his mirror and ask himself, *Do I look like one of the best salespeople in my branch?*

Look the Part

He was critical of himself, especially with regard to his dress and grooming. If he did not feel that he looked like a top salesperson, he would continue to make changes until he did. Only then would he go off to work. Within a year, he was one of the top salespeople in his branch. He only associated with the other top salespeople. He had become like them.

Moving Up

As a result of his high level of sales, he was invited to the national sales convention. At the convention, he made a point of going to each of the top salespeople from around the country sometime during the convention and asking for their advice. Not surprisingly, they were flattered, and told him some of the things that they had done to move from the bottom to the top of their field. When he got back home, he wrote them letters of thanks and put their ideas to work. His sales went up, up, and away.

Soon he was the top salesman in his branch, and later, the top salesman in the state. Over a period of five years, he transformed his life. At the national sales conventions, he was invited onto the stage to receive prizes and awards. By his eighth year in the business, he was the top salesman in the country.

What he told me was interesting. He said that all of his success had come from asking other top salespeople what they were doing and then following their guidance. But what he learned was that, even though these top salespeople had been going up on the stage and receiving prizes for sales excellence year after year, he was the *first* person who had ever sought them out and asked them for advice.

Fly with the Eagles

David McClelland of Harvard, author of *The Achieving Society*, observed that the major difference between success and failure in life is your choice of a "reference group."

He concluded that "birds of a feather flock together." The reference group, the group that you choose to associate with most of the time, largely determines what you accomplish in life. You tend to take on the values, attitudes, dress, and lifestyle of the people around you.

If you associate with *successful* people, you tend to adopt their attitudes, philosophies, manners of speaking and dress, work habits, and so on. In no time, you will start to get the results they do.

The Fatal Error
What McClelland also found was that the choice of a *negative* or unmotivated reference group could be enough in itself to condemn a person to lifelong underachievement and failure. A person could go to the best university, get the finest education, and have the greatest talents and abilities, but if he associated with *unsuccessful* people, he would be a failure as well.

What we have found is that a change in your reference group, moving from one company to another, or starting to associate with successful people, can transform your life and your results. But as Zig Ziglar said, "You can't fly with the eagles if you keep scratching with the turkeys."

Human beings are very much like chameleons. We take on the attitudes and behaviors of the people with whom we associate. We become like these people. We adopt their opinions. The power of suggestion, especially the outlooks and view of other people, exerts an enormous influence on how we think and feel about ourselves, and how we behave on a day-to-day basis.

7. Character Is Everything
Guard your integrity as a sacred thing. Nothing is more important to the quality of your life in our society. In business and sales success, you must have *credibility*. You can only be successful if people trust you and believe in you.

Guard your integrity as a sacred thing.

In study after study, the element of trust has been identified as the most important distinguishing factor between one salesperson and another, and one company and another.

As Stephen Covey says, "If you want to be trusted, be *trustworthy*." Honesty means that you always keep your word, and you always tell the truth.

Be True to Yourself

There is another element to integrity that is equally important. As Shakespeare said, "To thine own self be true, and then it must follow, as the night the day, thou canst not then be false to any man."

You must be true to yourself, to the very best that you know. You must live in truth with yourself and refuse to engage in self-delusion. You must be perfectly honest and not wish that things could or would be other than they are. Develop the ability to face the world and see life as it is, not as you wish it would be or could be.

Most people are pretty honest. They don't lie, cheat, or steal. They do their work, pay their taxes, and deal straightforwardly with others. But even the most honest people sometimes wish and hope and want to believe things that are not true.

Practice the Reality Principle

Jack Welch, president of General Electric, said that the most important principle in leadership is the "reality principle" and that this principle is based on the need to seek the truth, wherever it might lead. "Deal with the world as it is," he said, "not as you wish it would be."

Whenever he had to deal with a problem or difficulty at General Electric, his first question would be, "What's the reality?"

In your life, it is absolutely essential that you be true to yourself, and that you *live in* truth with yourself. It is vital that you be true to the best that is in you. You must do the things *every day* that lead to the goals you have set for yourself. Face the reality of your life, whatever it is. This is the mark of the truly honest person.

8. Unlock Your Inborn Creativity

Think of yourself as a highly intelligent person, even a *genius*. Recognize that you have great reserves of creativity that you have never used. Say aloud, over and over, "I'm a genius! I'm a genius! I'm a genius!"

This may sound like an exaggeration, but it isn't. The fact is that every person has the ability to perform at genius levels in one or more areas. You have within you, right now, the ability to do more and be more than you ever have before. You have the inborn capacity to exceed all your previous accomplishments. You have enormous reserves of creativity and intelligence. As Dennis Waitley says, "You have more potential than you could use in 100 lifetimes."

Use Your Inborn Talents

One of your foremost aims in life must be to identify your *special talents* and then to develop those talents to a high level. This is where your intelligence shines through. In testing, 95 percent of young children performed at genius levels. But when those same children were tested as adults, only 5 percent still performed with high levels of creativity and imagination. In the intervening years, they learn that, "if you want to get along, you have to go along."

The very best area of genius, or special talent for you, would be in the art of selling. Only about 10 percent of salespeople are completely suited to perform all seven of the key skills in selling at a high level. If this is the case for you, then you are virtually guaranteed a lifetime of high earnings and great professional success.

How to Detect Your Special Talents

There are several ways that you can detect your area of special talent. First, it is something that you *enjoy* doing. When you are not doing it, you think about it and about getting back to it.

Second, it is something that *absorbs your attention* completely. When you are doing what you are uniquely suited to do, you lose track of time. You often forget to eat, drink, or rest when you are doing what you are meant to do.

Third, you love to *learn about it* and become better at it throughout your life. You are hungry for books, audio programs, and courses that give you ideas to be even better in your area of special talent.

Fourth, you love to *talk about it*, discuss it, hear about it, and associate with people who are doing what you are ideally suited to do yourself.

Sometimes you hear people say, "When I am at work, I do my work. But when I leave work, I don't think about it at all." This type of person has a limited future in whatever he is doing. A person who does not think about his work when he is away from it is a person who is not suited to that line of work. If you are doing the right thing for you, your work and your personal life are interwoven, with only a thin dividing line between the two.

Fifth, and perhaps the best indication of your natural talent, is that it is something that is *easy to learn* and *easy to do*. In fact, you forget how you learned it in the first place; it was so easy for you. It seems to be a natural expression of your personality. You do it easily and well, almost without effort.

One of the reasons for underachievement is that many people consider themselves to be average rather than exceptional. They look at other people who are doing better than they are and assume that those people are better than they are. But if they think in that way, their logical con-clusion is that, if someone else is better, they must be worse. If someone else is worth more, they must be *worth less* (read "worthless"). This feel-ing of worthlessness and mediocrity can lead to an acceptance of average performance, even when they are really capable of superior performance.

9. Practice the Golden Rule

Practice the Golden Rule in all your interactions with others: Do unto others as you would have them do unto you.

Think about yourself as a customer. How would you like to be treated? Obviously, you would want a salesperson to be straightforward with you. You would want her to take the time to thoroughly understand your problem or need and then show you, step by step, how her solution could help you improve your life or work in a cost-effective way.

You would appreciate honesty and straight dealing. You would want the salesperson to explain the weaknesses as well as the strengths of her product. You would then want the salesperson to follow through on her promises and to fulfill her commitments to you. If this is what *you* would want from a salesperson selling to *you,* then be sure to give this to every customer you talk to.

The Universal Maxim

Practice the Universal Maxim of Emanuel Kant, the Dutch philoso-pher. He said, "Conduct your life as though your every act were to become a universal law for all people."

Imagine that everyone in your world was going to behave and treat every other person the way you did. When you set this as your standard for behavior, you will find yourself practicing the Golden Rule and treat-ing each person like a million-dollar client.

Ask yourself: *What kind of a company would my company be, if everyone in it were just like me?*

Imagine that each person who meets you is going to judge your entire company, management, products, services, guarantees and warranties, and follow-up support based on how you treated him or her, one on one. The mark of superior people is that they set high standards for themselves, and they refuse to compromise their standards. They imagine that everyone is watching them, even when no one is watching. You can tell the character of a person by what he does and how he carries himself when he is alone.

10. Pay the Price of Success

Finally, and perhaps more important than anything else, resolve to *work hard.* This is one of the great keys to success in life. In the background research for *The Millionaire Next Door,* Drs. Stanley and Danko interviewed thousands of self-made millionaires, asking them to what they attributed their success. An astounding 85 percent of self-made millionaires in America admitted that they were no more intelligent or talented than others, but that they "worked much harder" than anyone else, for a much longer time.

The key to success in selling is for you to start a little earlier, work a little harder, and stay a little later. Do the little things that average people always try to avoid doing. When you begin your workday, resolve to "work all the time you work." Don't waste time. Get going. Move fast. Develop a sense of urgency, a bias for action.

> **The key to success in selling is for you to start a little earlier, work a little harder, and stay a little later.**

Give It Full Throttle

Hard work and life success can be compared to taking off and flying an airplane. When you get into the plane and taxi to the end of the runway, you call the tower and request clearance for takeoff. As soon as you get your clearance, you give the plane full throttle, 100 percent, to move yourself down the runway and into the air.

Here is my point. If you only gave the plane 80 percent or even 90 percent throttle, you would never reach takeoff speed. You would stay on the ground until you ran out of runway and crashed.

Don't Hold Back

In life it is much the same. Many people work hard, but they do not work all out, with 100 percent commitment. As a result, they never reach the point of takeoff that puts them in the top 10 percent in their field. They always stay aground, among the average. They remain in the 80 percent of salespeople who only earn 20 percent of the money that's available.

The good news is that if you push your throttle on full and barrel down the runway, gaining speed and lift, you soon take off. By keeping your throttle wide open, you will climb and climb until you finally reach cruising altitude. Once you reach cruising altitude, you can pull back on the throttle, take it a little easier, and you will remain at that high altitude throughout your journey.

In your sales career, especially at the beginning, you must work all out, with 100 percent of your energy, to get free of the earth's gravity and break out of the pack of mediocrities. But once you reach your cruising altitude and get into the top 10 percent of money earners in your field, you can pull back on the throttle, spend more time with your family and friends, and still maintain your income and results at high levels.

Your Future Is Unlimited

You have within you, right now, the ability to be more, do more, and have more than you ever have in your life. By becoming absolutely excellent in your chosen profession of selling, you can achieve all your goals and fulfill all your dreams. You can create a wonderful life for yourself and your family. You can become one of the most valuable people in your company and industry. You can earn the respect and esteem of all the people around you. You can make a significant difference in the lives of your company, your customers, and your community. By learning and practicing the psychology of selling, you can reach the stars. And there are no limits.

ACTION
EXERCISES

1. Make a decision today to become one of the very best sales-people in your industry; pay any price, make any sacrifice, and never quit until you make it.

2. Dedicate yourself to lifelong learning; read, listen to audio programs, and attend seminars; your life only gets better when you get better.

3. Manage your time well; plan carefully in advance and resolve to make every minute count.

4. Do what you love to do; throw your whole heart into your work, and never stop getting better.

5. Resolve in advance that you are going to be a big success in life, and that you are never going to quit until you achieve your most important goals.

6. Sit down immediately and make a list of ten goals you would like to achieve in the next twelve months; select the most important goal on that list and work on it every day.

7. Work all the time you work; live at full throttle; start early, work harder, and stay later. Pay the price of success in full, in advance.

Nature cannot be tricked or cheated. She will give up to you the object of your struggles only after you have paid her price.

—NAPOLEON HILL

FOCAL POINT ADVANCED COACHING AND MENTORING PROGRAM

This intensive one-year program is ideal for ambitious, successful men and women who want to achieve better results and greater balance in their lives.

If you are already earning more than $100,000 per year and if you have a large degree of control over your time, in four full days with me in San Diego—one day every three months—you will learn how to double your productivity and income and double your time off with your family at the same time.

Every ninety days, you work with me and an elite group of successful entrepreneurs, self-employed professionals, and top salespeople for an entire day. During this time together, you form a "mastermind alliance" from which you gain ideas and insights that you can apply immediately to your work and personal life.

The Focal Point Advance Coaching and Mentoring Program is based on four areas of effectiveness: CLARIFICATION, SIMPLIFICATION, MAXIMIZATION, and MULTIPLICATION. You learn a series of methods and strategies to incorporate these principles into everything you do.

CLARIFICATION. You learn how to develop absolute clarity about who you really are and what you really want in each of seven key areas of life. You determine your values, vision, mission, purpose, and goals for yourself, your family, and your work.

SIMPLIFICATION. You learn how to dramatically simplify your life, getting rid of all the little tasks and activities that contribute little to the achievement of your real goals of high income, excellent family relationships, superb health and fitness, and financial independence. You learn how to streamline, delegate, outsource, minimize, and eliminate all those activities that are of little value.

MAXIMIZATION. You learn how to get the very most out of yourself by implementing the best time and personal management tools and techniques. You learn how to get more done in less time, how to increase your income rapidly, and how to have even more time for your personal life.

MULTIPLICATION. You learn how to leverage your special strengths to accomplish vastly more than you could by relying on your own efforts and resources. You learn how to use other people's money, other people's efforts, other people's ideas, and other people's customers and contacts to increase your personal productivity and earn more money.

Brian Tracy gives the Focal Point Advanced Coaching and Mentoring Program personally four times each year in San Diego. Each session includes complete pre-work, detailed exercises, and instruction, all materials, plus meals and refreshments during the day. At the end of each session, you emerge with a complete blueprint for the next ninety days.

If you are interested in attending this program, visit our website at www.briantracy.com, or phone our vice president, Victor Risling, at 1-800-542-4252 (ext. 17) to request an application form or more information. We look forward to hearing from you.

ABOUT THE
AUTHOR

Brian Tracy—Keynote Speaker, Consultant, Seminar Leader

Brian Tracy is a successful businessman and one of the top professional speakers in the world. He has started, built, managed, or turned around 22 different businesses. He addresses more than 250,000 people each year throughout the United States, Canada, Europe, Australia and Asia.

Brian's keynote speeches, talks and seminars are customized and tailored for each audience. They are described as "inspiring, entertaining, informative, and motivational." He has worked with more than 500 corporations, given more than 2,000 talks, and addressed over 2,000,000 people.

Some of his talks and seminars include:

LEADERSHIP IN THE NEW MILLENIUM—How to be a more effective leader in every area of business life. Learn the most powerful, practical leadership strategies ever discovered to manage, motivate, and get better results than ever before.

21ST CENTURY THINKING—How to outthink, outplan, and outperform your competition. Learn how to get superior results in a fast-moving, fast-changing business environment.

THE PSYCHOLOGY OF PEAK PERFORMANCE—How the top people think and act in every area of personal and business life. You learn a series of practical, proven methods and strategies for maximum achievement.

SUPERIOR SALES STRATEGIES—How to sell more, faster, and easier to demanding customers in highly competitive markets. There is a major difference between being a salesperson in business and being in business as a salesperson. Being successful in sales has a lot more to do with what's on the inside of a person, and the person's ability to establish and foster loyal relationships.

Brian will carefully customize his talk for you and your audience. Call today for full information on booking Brian to speak at your next meeting or conference. Visit www.briantracy.com, phone 858-481-2977, or write Brian Tracy International, 462 Stevens Avenue, Suite 202, Solana Beach, CA 92075.

OTHER OUTSTANDING BOOKS FOR SALESPEO-PLE

There is a major difference between being a salesperson in business and being in business as a salesperson. Being successful in sales has a lot more to do with what's on the inside of a person, and the person's ability to establish and foster loyal relationships.

This book gives a fresh understanding of the "laws" that govern the sales profession. The first section includes the laws that deal with the attitudes, aptitudes, and abilities that are required for any salesperson to be successful. The second section deals with the laws concerning the communication, courtship, camaraderie and commitments between a successful salesperson and his or her clients. Each law provides a description of a practical application. If you've ever held a sales position you know that being successful takes more than a smile, a Rolodex and a ""can do" attitude. This book provides the "more" you will need to come out on top and stay there.

ISBN: 0-7852-6393-4

Wall Street Journal and *Business Week* best-selling author and leader of one of America's top sales training companies, Todd Duncan reveals the 10 most deadly mistakes salespeople make, and offers insight on how to avoid them.

Three are approximThere are approximately 12.2 million salespeople in the United States—that's about 1 out of every 23 people! Salespeople are everywhere, selling everything imaginable. Some are making a killing, but a greater percentage end up victims of the sales industry—and their own mistakes. Some are normal bumps in the road toward success. Others are more damaging. But many are fatal to a career.

Duncan addresses these catastrophic mistakes with clarity and directness. Whether you're a seasoned sales professional or someone considering sales as a career, Duncan's wisdom can help you avoid errors in perception, practice, and performance that could not only kill a sale but also your career.

ISBN: 0-7852-6322-5

NEW YORK TIMES BESTSELLER
TODD DUNCAN
AUTHOR OF HIGH TRUST SELLING

TIME
TRAPS

PROVEN STRATEGIES FOR
SWAMPED PROFESSIONALS

Productivity. It has been a buzz word in the business world for years. But despite our best attempts and countless self-help books, we still fall behind, work late, juggle our schedules, and become swamped. *Time Traps* addresses the most common misconceptions we have about time and our use of that time in the marketplace. Duncan has proven remedies for universal time troubles, and he shows readers how to set a schedule that works not just some days but every day. With the principles in *Time Traps*, professionals will see a rise in their productivity as they experience a drop in their working hours.

ISBN: 0-7852-6323-3

CPSIA information can be obtained at www.ICGtesting.com
Printed in the USA
LVOW061433301012

305062LV00002B/8/P